SPORTS CAR

JAGUAR, FERRARI AND PORSCHE

ICONS

SPORTS CAR

JAGUAR, FERRARI AND PORSCHE
ICONS

WRITTEN BY

JOHN HEILIG, DENNIS ADLER, AND RANDY LEFFINGWELL

CRESTLINE

CRESTLINE

An imprint of MBI Publishing Company

This edition published in 2004 by Crestline, an imprint of MBI Publishing Company, Galtier Plaza, Suite 200, 380 Jackson Street, St. Paul, MN 55101-3885 USA

Jaguar © John Heilig, 1997, 2004
Ferrari © Dennis Adler, 1997, 2004
Porsche © Randy Leffingwell, 1995, 2004

Crestline titles are also available at discounts in bulk quantity for industrial or sales-promotional use. For details write to Special Sales Manager at Motorbooks International Wholesalers & Distributors, Galtier Plaza, Suite 200, 380 Jackson Street, St. Paul, MN 55101-3885 USA.

ISBN 0-7603-1777-1

Cover design by Koechel Peterson & Associates, Minneapolis, Minnesota

Printed in China

Front cover: With the debut of a replacement for the F 512 M (Testarossa), Ferrari has closed the circle giving the firm a new car in every V-8 and V-12 category from Berlinetta and Spider to GT 2+2, thus marking the beginning of Ferrari's second half century.

Front banner (left to right): (#1) Special instrumentation was added to the 1990 Porsche 930 Turbo Cabrio Flatnose, some adapted from race cars, others from air craft. A moisture sensor will raise the top and windows, arm the alarm, and notify the owner by remote pager of the change in weather.

(#2) The 1966 XJ13 concept car was designed by Malcolm Sayer and was a mid-engine configuration with a similarity to the E-type and other sports-racing cars of the era such as the Lola/Ford GT40 and McLaren-Elva.

(#3) The 40th anniversary Ferrari, the F40, became one of the most speculative models in Ferrari history. At a suggested retail price of $250, 000, the limited-edition cars soared to nearly $1 million as speculators and investors traded them like commodities until the sports car market crashed.

(#4) Ironically, critics called the stainless steel 1972 Typ 911S Targa too flashy.

On the title page:
Last of the 308-derived V-8 sports cars, the Ferrari 328GT Berlinetta and Spyder carried the same body lines in both the European and American versions.

On the back cover, top: The SS100, introduced in 1935, was the first sport car introduced by Swallow. At this time, William Lyons was thinking of a new name for his company. Later versions of the SS100 would reflect that name—Jaguar.
Bottom: The engine in the 250 GT Cabriolet Series I was a Colombo-designed 60-degree V-12.

CONTENTS

JAGUAR

FERRARI

PORSCHE

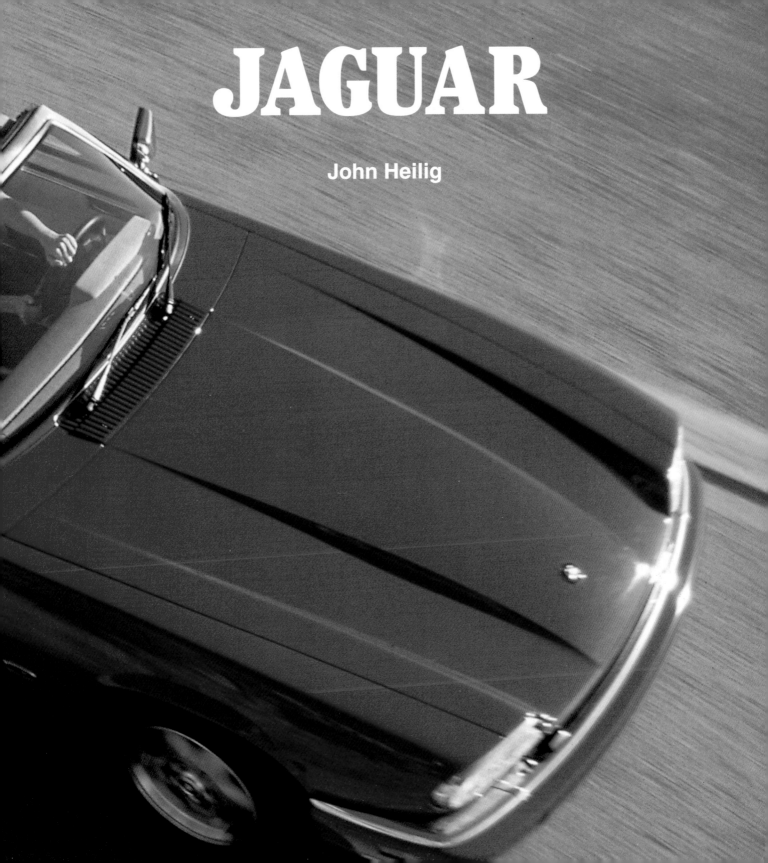

JAGUAR

John Heilig

Acknowledgments

William Lyons was a genius. He had the foresight to create a product—initially assembling that product out of readily available components—that the public fell in love with and bought. With the profits gained from these simple products, he developed more complex products and established an automobile company that has persisted for over 70 years.

That company, of course, is Jaguar. And while Lyons began by building motorcycle sidecars with his neighbor, William Walmsley, the cars he created toward the end of his life were exotic sports cars and luxury sedans that had no equal in the world.

Like most youths of the 1950s, I loved the legend of Jaguar. I had an MG budget, but a Jaguar was always the goal. Eventually, I was able to buy an aged 3.4 sedan (for $300) that at least brought me some of the thrill of owning the sports cars. But despite the fact that the 3.4 appeared to have been built with quarter-inch-thick steel in the fenders, the transmission was fragile and broke. I wasn't up to attempting the repairs or restoration, so I traded it in on a more practical economy car.

Today, the products of Jaguar are luxury sedans and one of the best sports cars in the world, the XK8. Things haven't changed much over the last 45 years. In 1989, Ford stepped in and rescued what is one of the last bastions of a once-thriving British automobile industry. The company that has survived after the Ford take-over is not emasculated, as many feared. It is, instead, stronger than ever and retains a level of independence that permits it to continue to develop its sedans and sports cars with a distinctly British flavor.

Many people helped in this project, most particularly Chris Gennone of Communication Dynamics International, who was its catalyst and who provided support, fact-checking and editorial assistance. Another source of great moral, editorial and photographic support was Len Alcaro of Jaguar Cars North America, who checked the manuscript and also made cars available to photograph.

Special thanks must be given to Don Vorderman, who graciously allowed me to use portions of his unpublished work on Bill Lyons. Also, thanks to Margaret Harrison for her photographs and to the Automobile Quarterly Photo and Research Library for supplying photographs when the original source dried up.

Car owners whose vehicles are in here include the late Jim Spooner, and Les Jackson, Jaguar Cars of North America,

As with anything I do, this couldn't have been completed without the love and support of my wife, Florence, our three daughters, Susan, Sharon and Laura, and their honeys. Well, it could have been completed, but it wouldn't have been worth it.

The Prewar Years

Chapter One

There would never have been a Jaguar car if there had never been a William Lyons. And Lyons might never have begun his life's work if there had not been a William Walmsley. Lyons, who was eventually to be knighted for his work with Jaguar, was designer, engineer, visionary and activist for Jaguar and the companies that would precede it. When he retired in 1972, the company lost its driving force and spirit, and lost its way for a couple of years. That it has been able to revive itself in the past 25 years is a credit to the organization that Lyons created and the men who worked so hard to save it, particularly John Egan, who would also be knighted.

1932 SS1 FIXED HEAD COUPE
The SS1 was the first full automobile built by William Lyons and William Walmsley. Introduced in October 1931, the SS1 had a modified 6-cylinder Standard chassis supplied by John Black of the Standard Motor Company. The underslung frame provided for a low body. Lyons wanted a body that was even lower than the production car, but Walmsley signed off on the slightly higher version when Lyons was in the hospital with appendicitis.

Don Vorderman, former editor of *Automobile Quarterly*, said of Lyons: "Had he done nothing else but serve as chief stylist at Jaguar, had he done nothing more than supervise the development of the SS100, or the XK120, or the prewar or postwar saloons, his place in the pantheon of automotive design would be secure. The remarkable fact is that he did all of these cars and a dozen or so more while simultaneously directing the operations of a major automobile company.

"A varied assortment of talents were present, all functioning smoothly and independently within him. Lyons' exquisite sense of design was merely one, but perhaps the most evident of his gifts. He also oversaw the engineering and advertising departments. He orchestrated their racing programs. He was a diplomat, too, having to deal with unions and successive governments that were all too often inclined to interfere with this or that aspect of his business.

"Of course he didn't create these legendary designs entirely on his own. There were a number

William Lyons' love of motorcycles is what led to the formation of Jaguar Cars. Lyons met William Walmsley, who had established a small factory to build motorcycle sidecars in the garage behind his home. Lyons bought a sidecar from Walmsley, and the two decided to go into business together to make sidecars. They grew the business to include building of custom bodies for Austin chassis, and eventually began designing their own cars on Standard chassis. From these Standard Swallows the Jaguar was born.

of talented people to assist him, most notably Malcolm Sayer, but while he was there, Bill Lyons had the first and last word on the design of every car Jaguar built." But we're getting ahead of ourselves.

William Lyons was born September 4, 1901, in the village of Blackpool. His father was an Irish musician who visited Blackpool one year as a member of an orchestra that was hired for holiday entertainment. Lyons Sr. never returned home, because he met and fell in love with a local girl,

Minnie. They were married and William Sr. opened a music store and sold pianos. When William Jr. was born, his father's music business was well-established.

As a youth, Lyons apprenticed at Crossley Motors Ltd. When he was 18, he began working for Brown and Mallalieu, a local car dealer, as a junior salesman.

Like most youths of the era, Lyons liked motorcycles. England had not yet been blessed with a "people's car" like the Model T Ford, so young dandies from middle-class families would buy motorcycles and attach sidecars as basic transportation.

Lyons first met William Walmsley when Walmsley's family moved into the same Blackpool neighborhood. Walmsley had been developing a small business in the family garage building sidecars for motorcycles. Lyons, who had owned an early Harley-Davidson, discovered Walmsley's business and bought a sidecar. The two eventually decided to join forces in 1922, but Lyons was still under the legal age of 21 required to acquire loans from banks. They had to wait until September 4, 1922, before founding the Swallow Sidecar Company with £1000 (around $5,000). The factory was at 7-9 Bloomfield Rd., in Blackpool.

Swallow Sidecars built as many as 10 zeppelin-shaped sidecars a week, fitted to chassis built by Montgomery's of Coventry. The most expensive chassis they sold cost £30.

In 1924, the same year Lyons married Greta Brown, Tourist Trophy entrants with Swallow sidecars finished second, third, and fourth in the annual motorcycle race on the Isle of Man.

Two years later, the company moved to larger premises in Cocker Street. It changed its name to the Swallow Sidecar & Coach Building Company because they had begun offering repairs to auto-

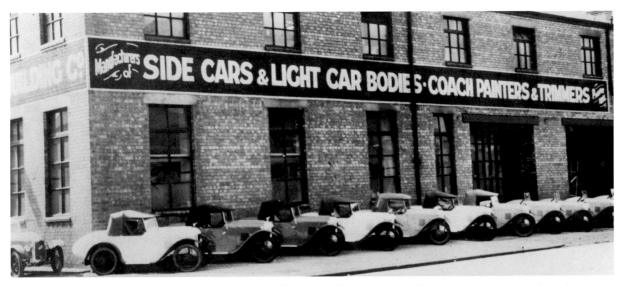

The original Swallow factory was in Blackpool, where "side cars and light car bodies" were manufactured, and coaches were painted and trimmed. The small Austin Swallows are lined up in front of the factory, showing their trim bodies that attracted someone who wanted the economy of an Austin Seven but not its utilitarian looks.

mobile bodies. This was all in preparation for a new business that would commence in January 1927, but which began with the introduction of the Austin Seven in 1922.

The Austin Seven was a genuine British car for the mass market, but it also proved to be a very good chassis on which to build custom bodies. Called the Seven because of its taxable horsepower, the little Austin was simple in design and execution. Lyons knew that he could buy a chassis for little money and could build a custom-bodied car for a reasonable asking price. The factory cars were also plain and wouldn't provide any competition for a custom design.

Lyons and Walmsley bought an Austin Seven chassis in 1927 for £100 and built their first car, designed by Lyons. It was a two-seater sports model with a top that was hinged at the rear. When this application proved to be awkward in the wind, the hinging was moved to the front for production models. Success of the Austin Swallow

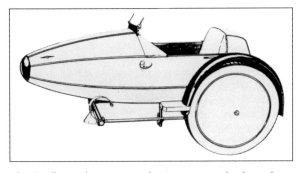

The Swallow sidecars were aluminum, torpedo-shaped and relatively aerodynamic. They provided the youth of the 1920s with a means of transporting themselves and a companion, since there was no equivalent of the inexpensive Model T Ford in England at the time. Later, the Austin Seven would serve that purpose, so Lyons was fortunate that he was born at the right time.

was assured when Henley's of London, a large Austin dealer, ordered 500 cars.

In mid-1928, a four-door Swallow sedan joined the lineup, also built on an Austin Seven chassis. Once again, the company changed its name, to the Swallow Coachbuilding Company,

1935 SS1 AIRLINE SALOON
Before they were Jaguars, William Lyons built the SS1, which was the first car totally designed by the Swallow Coachbuilding Company, predecessor to Jaguar. The SS1 was built on a modified 6-cylinder Standard chassis, supplied to Lyons and William Walmsley for this purpose. With a low-slung chassis and the engine set back 7 inches from where it was in the Standard, stylish bodies were possible. This body is an Airline Saloon, or sedan. Airline designs were the fastbacks of the 1930s, and similar products from companies such as MG remain stylish to today. *Margaret Harrison*

indicating future intent. Swallow still built motorcycle sidecars, and would through World War II, but automobiles would play a larger and larger role in the company's affairs.

"The (Swallow) bodies were attractive," wrote Ken Purdy. "They ran to split windshields, external sun visors, wire wheels, and good options in two-tone paint jobs—but the running gear under them was never up to the performance the coachwork seemed to promise."

In November 1928, Swallow moved to Coventry, England, in the center of the British automobile industry. It was the equivalent of a new American automobile manufacturer moving its operations to Detroit. The building was an old artillery shell-filling factory.

Swallow built cars on chassis supplied by Austin, Wolseley, Morris, Swift, Standard and the Fiat 509. Eventually, designs on the Morris chassis were abandoned when Morris began building a more sporty version of its own cars and called it MG.

In May 1931, John Black, managing director of the Standard Motor Company, agreed to sell a modified 6-cylinder Standard chassis to Swallow for the creation of Swallow's first total design, the SS1. Standard agreed to modify the

1936 SS1 AIRLINE DROPHEAD COUPE
SS Cars Ltd. built several body variations on the SS1 chassis. This Drophead Coupe is what is referred to in the United States as a convertible, with a removable top. Some drophead coupes had landau irons framing the C-pillar area of the top, but in the case of the SS1, the top is simpler. The Airline coupes were powered by 2,143 and 2,663 side valve 6-cylinder engines that were derived from the Standard 16 and Standard 20, respectively. *Margaret Harrison*

1936 SS1 AIRLINE SALOON
This SS1 Airline Saloon has a different rear treatment than the 1935 SS1 Airline Saloon. The rear styling is more conventional, with a square addition to the body for the trunk. *Margaret Harrison*

1934 SS1
By the time the 1934 SS1 was produced, the wheelbase had been extended 7 inches. The company had gone public in 1933, and co-founder William Walmsley had left. Lyons was in full control now, and the roofline of the 1934 SS1 reflected his taste more.

chassis by adding 3 inches to the wheelbase and stuffing in a higher axle ratio for more top speed—but of course, less acceleration. The frame was underslung and the engine was set back 7 inches. The first SS1 cars were introduced in October 1931 at the London Motor Show, along with the SS2, which was essentially an SS1 with a 30-inch shorter chassis. Incidentally, nobody is certain as to the exact meaning of "SS," since it was never well-defined. It could have stood for "Swallow Sports," "Standard Swallow," or "Swallow Side-car," but neither Lyons nor Walmsley ever revealed what they were thinking.

Vorderman, an owner of numerous Jaguars, wrote, "It was with the announcement of the SS1 late in 1931, based on still another manufacturer's running gear, that Lyons burst out of obscurity to become one of the most respected figures in the British automobile business, a position he would occupy with dignity and grace for the rest of his life."

"The SS1 of 1932 knocked the British industry on its collective ear," Vorderman continued, "offering what journalists began calling 'The car with the 1,000 pound look'—that's nearly the price of a contemporary Bentley chassis—but it cost only £310. It was about that time that people began asking each other the question that would follow Jaguars around for years to come, 'How can they do it for the money?' The truth is that there was a great deal of profit to be made in the building and selling of coachbuilt motorcars in those days. In creating the SS1, Lyons had simply selected a proven, inexpensive chassis from the Standard Motor Company, had it slightly modified to his own specifications and then set up a production line to mass produce handbuilt bodies for it, hundreds at a time. Simple."

The SS1 was known primarily for its style, rather than its performance. Both the coupe and two-door sedan had long hoods, flowing fenders, wire wheels and low rooflines. Actually, Lyons wanted a roofline that was even lower than the one that appeared on the cars, but Walmsley signed off on a more practical version when Lyons was in the hospital with appendicitis.

Based on the Standard 16 horsepower chassis, it was officially known as the SS Sixteen. Later, a larger 20 horsepower engine was also offered.

In 1933, the company's name was changed again, to SS Cars Ltd. William Lyons was named Chairman and Managing Director. In 1934, he proposed going public with the company. William Walmsley didn't share Lyons' ambition, and resigned amicably, turning total control of SS Cars over to Lyons. Walmsley was a practical engineer who was as happy tinkering with his model railroad trains as he was with cars.

The 1933 version of the SS1 had a 7-inch longer wheelbase and an underslung chassis, which gave a lower seating position and the lower roofline that Lyons had originally wanted.

The shorter SS2 that appeared at the same time as the SS1 was known as the "little brother" to the bigger car. The car was powered by 9, 10 and 12 horsepower Standard engines. The SS2 retained some of the panache of the bigger car, albeit in a more compact fashion.

Lyons introduced his first sports model, the SS90, early in 1935. It was soon followed by the more powerful SS100. Between the introductions, Lyons was also hard at work thinking of a new name for the cars. One of the names he considered was "Sunbeam," but the Rootes organization had secured the rights to that name. "Jaguar" was eventually chosen. But first, Lyons had to obtain permission from Armstrong-Siddely, another Coventry firm that had a tradition of giving big cat names to their airplane engines—Cougar, Cheetah and Lynx, for example.

The first car to carry that name, SS Jaguar, was a sedan version of the SS90 with wire wheels. A Tourer version of the car was also introduced in 1935. In September, the SS Jaguar 100 was advertised as "an entirely new SS for 1936." Priced at £385 ($1,900), and available in 1½ (1608cc) and 2½ (2662cc) liter versions, it generated more than 100 horsepower with the larger engine.

The extra power was derived from a head design by Harry Weslake, who was England's greatest expert on cylinder head design and who was working as a consultant to Lyons. His overhead valve head for the Standard six increased the power of the 2.6-liter engine from 70 to 100 horsepower. Working for Jaguar as chief engineer was William Heynes, who joined the company in 1935.

British writer John Stanford, in *The Sports Car*, said in 1962 of the first cars to bear the Jaguar name: "The introduction . . . of the first Jaguar series saw the beginnings of a really well-merited rise to spectacular success. Like the modern Jaguars, they were the work of William M. Heynes; and had very robust pushrod o.h.v. engines, well-chosen gear ratios, and rigid, rather stiffly sprung chassis. From the beginning, an open short-chassis version was available with 2½- or 3½-liter engine, at a very low price. The opulent and slightly flashy

1937 SS100
The SS100, introduced in 1935, was the first sport car introduced by Swallow. At this time, William Lyons was thinking of a new name for his company. Later versions of the SS100 would reflect that name—Jaguar. The SS100 was available in 1 1/2- and 2 1/2-liter versions, with the latter generating more than 100 horsepower. An SS100 could go 100 miles per hour, and the car was victorious in many races, hillclimbs and rallies.

lines, with their rakish swept wings and exaggerated long bonnets, have dated somewhat to modern eyes; and with the engine well forward in the very short chassis, handling was apt to leave some room for improvement. None the less, performance was available in full measure, both versions having top speeds closely approaching 100 miles per hour with considerable refinement."

American writer Ken Purdy wrote: "The SS1 and SS2 passenger cars were backed up by sports models—SS90, SS100—because Lyons, whose grasp of the fundamentals has never been less than brilliant, knew that competition effort was vital to sales, particularly in Europe and particularly then. A good SS100 would do 100 miles per hour and the model had notable successes in rallies, hill climbs, and sports car races. An SS100 won the International Alpine Trial of 1936 (and again in 1948) and the 1937 Royal Automobile Club Rally. The car would not only run, it had visual appeal to burn—a happy amalgam of the design points that were the desiderata of the day: big flat-lens headlights, flaring fenders, louvers all over the hood, curved dashboard carrying saucer-sized main instruments, a saddle gas tank hung astern. Only a few SS100s were made and the survivors are all classics." Tommy Wisdom and his wife Elsie (or "Bill") won the 1934 Alpine Trial in a factory-sponsored car.

In 1937, a 3½-liter version of the SS Jaguar 100 was introduced and immediately earned its stripes in competition. Sammy Newsome set the fastest time at the Shelsley Walsh hill climb in a 3½-liter SS100. Tommy Wisdom won the Long Handicap race at Brooklands in the same car.

"The SS100 is certainly one of the best looking sports cars ever built," wrote Don Vorderman. "Its swooping wings, extremely low build, its long, louvered bonnet, excellent cockpit and lavish instrumentation were the perfect expression of the sports car of the 1930s. The fact that it wasn't nearly as fast as it looked and had whimsical mechanical brakes seemed to have little effect on people's enthusiasm for it. A little more than 300 SS100s were made from 1936 into 1940, and according to the Jaguar Register, most of them are still around, arousing lustful thoughts among a new generation of car fanciers and appreciating at a dizzying rate."

For the 1938 model year, SS Jaguar sedans changed from wood frames to all-steel construction. The 3½-liter engine joined the sedan lineup that year as well. In a trend away from sportiness, the spare tire was moved from its location on the fender to under the floor of the trunk.

Purdy: "To give the first SS Jaguar the performance its appearance called for, Lyons had asked the designer Harry Weslake to modify Standard's side-valve engine into an overhead-valve unit and had brought in W.M. Heynes to oversee engineering, the beginning of an enduring association with the company for both men. Heynes was a vice-chairman when he retired, full of honors, in 1969. Like the SS1 that had gone before it, the new SS Jaguar sedan looked more expensive than it was: a poll of dealers at its introduction showed an average price guess of £632 ($3,000), but the sticker was only £385 ($1885). The model was another smash success (it was called the poor man's Bentley, sometimes admiringly, sometimes not), and when everything stopped for World War II in September 1939, the firm was turning out 250 cars a week."

Jaguar's oldest established American dealership opened in 1938. Hugh Weidinger's Hempstead Motors on Long Island in New York became an imported car dealership that year and continues today, despite the death in 1995 of its founder. Hempstead Motors sells Jaguars and Mercedes-Benz today, among others but not in the same showroom.

As the 1930s drew to a close, SS Cars Ltd. was a growing company whose products had developed a strong following in England and had earned recognition in the United States as well. Unfortunately, that growth would be put on hold for six years when Great Britain declared war on Germany on September 3, 1939. SS Cars continued to use its remaining stocks of raw materials to build cars as late as the spring of 1940. In the last full year of car production before switching over to war production.

The
1940s

Chapter Two

During the war, Swallow Sidecars, which was still a subsidiary of SS Cars, made more than 10,000 sidecars for British army motorcycles. In addition, the company built 50,000 trailers for the war effort in three different weight classes. Before hostilities began, SS had begun building wing tips for Stirling bombers. Another major effort was the repair and modification of Armstrong Whitworth "Whitley" bombers. Planes would be trucked to the Foleshill plant, where they would be repaired. After repairs were completed, they would be trucked to a local

airfield for tests. When the Whitley was taken out of service, SS repaired the "Welington." The company also made components for the Supermarine "Spitfire," Avro "Lancaster," DeHavilland "Mosquito" and Airspeed "Oxford" planes. As the war wound down, SS also built the complete center section of the Gloster "Meteor," which was England's first operational jet-powered fighter.

Toward the end of the war, Walter Hassan, who had joined SS cars from Bentley in 1938, and Claude Bailey designed two lightweight vehicles that were to be parachuted into battle. Called the VA and VB, they were both built with unibody construction and had 4-wheel independent suspensions. The VA was powered by a rear-mounted 1096 JAP motorcycle engine with chain drive. The VB had a Ford 10 horsepower engine and used a 3-speed transmission in a more conventional layout. Because of its rear-mounted engine, the VA had excellent traction, and the front end could be lifted by one man. Neither car pro-

1948 JAGUAR MARK IV DROPHEAD COUPE
The 1948 "Mark IV" Jaguar sedans and Drophead coupes were postwar versions of the prewar 3 1/2-, 2 1/2- and 1 1/2- liter versions. Although never officially recognized as the Mark IV by the factory, the postwar versions of these cars acquired these names. This Mark IV was powered by a 3 1/2-liter inline 6-cylinder engine that was soon overshadowed by the 6-cylinder XK engine that Jaguar had been developing during the war. This Drophead Coupe was capable of a top speed of 90 miles per hour.

1947 JAGUAR MK IV SEDAN
The first cars Jaguar built after the war were pre-war designs, the Mark IV 3 1/2-liter sedan. This Australian example shows the big headlights typical of pre-war cars, combined with a decidedly vertical architecture, as exemplified by the grille. The sweeping front fenders connect all the way to the rear, offering vestiges of running boards. *Margaret Harrison*

ceeded beyond the prototype stage because the development of transport aircraft went so quickly that it was possible for them to carry heavier loads, and air-drop full-sized Jeeps into battle, rather than specially designed lightweight vehicles.

Because of its location in England's industrial sector, Coventry received a lot of attention from German bombers. The center of the city was the focus of several Luftwaffe blitzkrieg raids. Ken Purdy wrote: ". . . the cathedral in Coventry, England. It had been burned and blown into rubble (during a ten-hour raid) on the night of November 14, 1940, by 500 Luftwaffe bombers in the longest raid England took during the war. Work to rebuild began the

All Jaguar sedans throughout the history of the company have exhibited long hoods, flowing fenders and short rear decks. This 1947 Mark IV 3 1/2-liter Sedan is typical of prewar designs converted to early postwar production. This angle also shows the semaphore turn signals, recessed door handles for both front and rear doors, and the wire wheels so beloved by William Lyons. *Margaret Harrison*

next day, the architect Sir Basil Spence planning the new cathedral on the site of the old, forming some of the standing ruins into it; the cornerstone was laid by the queen sixteen years and a bit later."

As for Jaguar, Browns Lane, 3 miles away from the cathedral, was only badly damaged once. Part of the roof of a newly constructed building on

Swallow Road was damaged. Don Vorderman recounts part of Jaguar's legend that has "Lyons and his chief engineer Bill Heynes . . . on air raid watches during World War II, mapping out their postwar plans. At times the obstacles must have seemed nearly insurmountable, with Coventry all but obliterated by the ten-hour air raid. The plan-

1947 JAGUAR MK IV SEDAN
Jaguars, especially the sedans, have featured the "leaper" hood ornament. Safety legislation of the 1980s dictated that such "unsafe" ornamentation should be removed to prevent injury to pedestrians. The leaper remains on select Jaguar sedans of the 1990s. *Margaret Harrison*

Part of the tradition of Jaguar cars has been the wood trim and leather upholstery. Wood-trimmed dash fascias date back to the earliest days of the company, as evidenced in this 1947 Mk IV sedan that was essentially a prewar car rushed into postwar production. This right-hand-drive Australian model also shows some interesting remnants of prewar design, such as the crank to open the bottom of the windshield, and a starter that is separate from the ignition. This car has been modified with the addition of a modern sound system. *Margaret Harrison*

ning continued, and when peace finally came, Jaguar was ready, though unfortunately the rest of the country was not." The company emerged from the war with a larger factory, expanded to increase war production.

One of Lyons' first actions as the war drew to its inevitable conclusion was to change the name of his company once again. SS Cars wasn't a popular name because "SS" had developed a strongly negative reputation during the war, thanks to Hitler's storm troopers (Schutzstaffel). Lyons responded by changing the name to Jaguar Cars Ltd., the name by which it has been known, in one form or another, for over half a century.

His next move was to get out of the sidecar business. Swallow Sidecars was sold, making Jaguar an automobile company once and for all.

Tube Investments bought the Swallow name, and continued producing sidecars until 1956, when it was absorbed by Watsonian, a Birmingham company that also made sidecars and had supplied William Walmsley with his first chassis in 1920. In the mid-1950s, Tube Investments dabbled briefly in the production of the Swallow Doretti sports car.

Lyons' final move was to buy the tooling that built the Standard 2½ and 3½-liter engines, making Jaguar a complete manufacturer. New equipment would be used to build the XK engines that were designed during the war.

The British government decreed that in order for manufacturers to obtain the raw materials necessary to return to production, 50 percent of that production must be exported. Car manufacturers in particular were urged to build vehicles for

Proper sedans of the 1930s carried fully equipped tool sets. In the case of the 1947 Jaguar Mk IV, which was a prewar design rushed into postwar production, the tool kit was included in the trunk and had the tools fitted into the case. Of interest, besides the important tire iron, screwdrivers, wrenches and hammer for wire wheel knock-offs, there is a pump to inflate tires, an oil can, and wire-cutter pliers. *Margaret Harrison*

export, especially to the United States, which was cash rich. Consequently, Jaguar added left-hand-drive cars to the mix late in 1945.

Jaguar was one of the first British manufacturers to return to production and was under way in July 1945. The first cars were modified prewar models. It wasn't until 1948 that a new model was introduced, the Mark V, which was available in sedan or convertible form with a 2½- or 3½-liter engine. This was the first Jaguar with independent front suspension and hydraulic brakes. As Ken Purdy wrote, "It was no ball of fire in performance and it had irritating detail flaws (for one, a heater

that couldn't cope with a brisk autumn day in Connecticut, never mind a Minnesota winter)." People loved the car anyway.

In 1946, Frank Raymond Wilton "Lofty" England joined Jaguar as service manager. He earned his nickname because of his height. England would lend his considerable organizational skills to Jaguar's racing program in the 1950s and would eventually become managing director of the company.

Lyons traveled to the United States for five weeks in 1948, appointing sales and service agents for Jaguar cars. With the government's export policies and Jaguar's potential for sales in the U.S.,

1948 JAGUAR MARK IV DROPHEAD COUPE
Besides the Saloon, or sedan, Jaguar also built Drophead coupe versions of the Mark IV. Still carried over from the prewar version of the car, the Drophead Coupe offered open-air driving. When compared with the SS1 Airlines, the grilles of the Mark IV Drophead Coupes seem taller and more massive. This is true, as the cars themselves were bigger. All were powered by the 2,663 cc 6-cylinder engine, that was now a Jaguar engine, since the factory that built the engines had been taken over from Standard by Jaguar. Note the large headlights, smaller "fog" lights, running lights on the fenders and landau irons on the top. *Margaret Harrison*

establishment of these agents was a smart move. Max Hoffman on the East Coast and Charles Hornburg on the West Coast were named the U.S. distributors. At the time, Jaguar sold 238 cars in the United States in 1948 and 158 in 1949. This was in an imported car market of 15,442 and 11,858, respectively. Incidentally, all the cars imported in those years were either British or French.

All the efforts of the company were not devoted entirely to the war during the struggle. William Heynes, who joined the company in 1935 as chief engineer, and Walter Hassan spent some of their time developing a new engine that would be used in Jaguar cars after the war. They worked on developing these "X" or experimental engines and were up to "XK" when they found a design they felt would work, a double overhead camshaft 6-cylinder of approximately 3.4 liters capacity. The XK engine proved to be the basis of Jaguar engines for more than 30 years after the end of hostilities.

The engine that Heynes and Hassan developed during the war was initially intended for a

This Australian Mark IV Drophead Coupe differs from the black one in that this car has the running lights on the fenders and the rear-view mirrors have been moved from the fender tops to the doors, where they are more practical. Both cars exhibit classic prewar Jaguar styling, with long flowing front fenders sweeping back to the rear fenders, which allows vestiges of running boards on both sides. *Margaret Harrison*

new sedan, which was to be a successor to the Mark V, but the new sedan wasn't ready in time. Therefore, Lyons and crew installed the engine in an aluminum-bodied sports car that was intended to be a stopgap low production vehicle. Since it had the 3.4-liter XK engine and engineers figured the car was capable of a top speed in the neighborhood of 120 miles per hour, it was named "XK120." The car was introduced in October 1948 at the London Motor Show. To confirm the car's potential—and its name—test driver Ron Sutton took an XK120 to the Jabbeke autoroute in Belgium (a favorite high-speed test track for auto companies) and traveled 132.596 miles per hour over the measured mile. Actor Clark Gable was one of the first buyers of an XK120 after he met Lyons at a cocktail party in Hollywood. In his bylined article in the May 1950 *Road & Track* he claimed to have driven the car 124 miles per hour.

As John Stanford wrote in *The Sports Car*, "That such an engine could be made in large numbers at a relatively low price, and also run, as some have done, for 100,000 miles without over-

1949 JAGUAR MK V
Jaguar introduced the "interim" Mark V sedan when the XK engine that was supposed to go into it was still not ready for production. Hence, the Mark V was powered by the older 3 1/2- and 3 1/2-liter engines that were based on the old prewar Standard engines. What was most significant about the Mark V, though, was its modern chassis, an independent front suspension. The Mark V used 16-inch wheels rather than the 18-inch wheels of its predecessor. Styling was slightly more modern than the Mark IV, with headlights fared into the fenders.

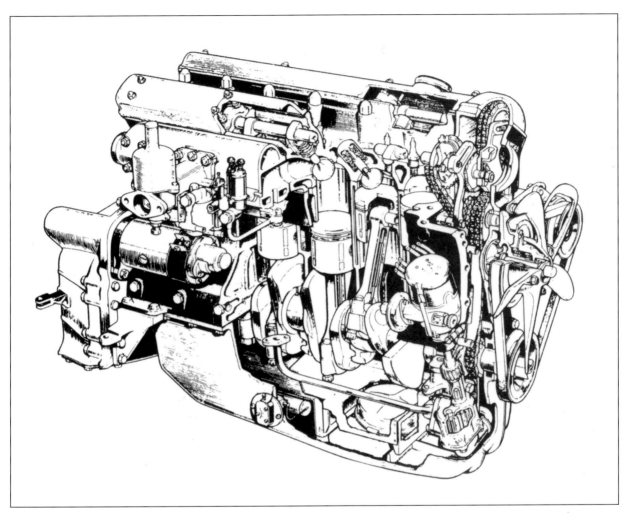

In 1948, Jaguar introduced the 3.4-liter double overhead cam 6-cylinder "XK" engine that would transform the company from building modified cars on another's chassis with Jaguar engines, into a full-scale automobile manufacturer. The XK engine had been designed by Lyons, Chief Engineer William Heynes, engine designers Walter Hassan and Claude Bailey while they were on fire watch duty during World War II on the roof of the factory in Coventry.

haul is perhaps the greatest proof of the advances made in design and production in that era."

The XK engine had a bore and stroke of 83 x 106 mm for a capacity of 3,442 cc. and delivered 120 bhp at 5,000 rpm. In experimental form it ran for 24 hours at 5,000 rpm with occasional bursts to as high as 6,000 rpm. The engine's strength may be attributed to the robust and large-diameter seven-bearing crankshaft and the reliability of the valve gear, with two chain-driven camshafts operating two valves per cylinder.

This engine was installed in a box-section frame with great torsional rigidity. The front suspension incorporated torsion bars, while the rear

used semi-elliptic leaf springs. On the first cars, a V-shaped windshield was fitted, but a small "aero screen" was available for racing. In the rear was a nice-sized luggage compartment, although a 25-gallon fuel tank could be fitted in place of the original equipment 15-gallon tank for longer runs.

After Jaguar built 240 cars with aluminum bodies and demand for the XK120 was still strong, the company switched to steel bodies. In all, from 1948 to 1953 when the XK120 was replaced by the XK140, more than 18,000 were built, with less than 600 going to the home market, confirming the government's export policy.

A 2.4-liter 4-cylinder version of the XK engine was also planned, with the idea of installing it in a "XK100" sports car, but the car was never built. The engine was developed later.

XK120s proved their worth on race tracks. One of the first recorded victories for the car was in the 1949 *Daily Express* race at Silverstone, when Leslie Johnson won and Peter Walker finished second. Johnson also drove the XK120 to its first sig-nificant U.S. success in 1950 when he finished second to George Huntoon's Ford-Duesenberg Special in the SCCA's Palm Beach races. John Fitch, who would go on to success as a Mercedes-Benz team driver, was a class winner at Bridgehampton in an XK120 in 1950, as was Erwin Goldschmidt at Westhampton. In June 1950, Clark and Haines finished 12th in Jaguar's first Le Mans effort.

One significant victory, for both car and driver, occurred in August 1950, when a young Stirling Moss won the Tourist Trophy race in Northern Ireland. Here was a major victory for the car and an equally important win for the driver who was soon to make his mark as one of the greatest racing drivers in history.

Jaguar finally introduced the Mark VII sedan (there was no Mark VI because Bentley had a model by that name) with the 3.4-liter XK engine at the London Motor Show in October 1950. When the car was later put on display at the New York Auto Show, dealers placed more than $20 million in orders.

JAGUAR
Mark VII

S4170
*At ports of entry;
sales tax, white-wall tires,
automatic transmission
and license extra.*

*Now with
automatic transmission*

Now the distinguished continental lines and superlative performance
of the Jaguar are enhanced by the simple utility of the automatic transmission.

Exclusively designed for Jaguar by Borg-Warner, this automatic transmission adds a final
note of distinction to a car already acclaimed for old-world craftsmanship and sports car performance.

Visit your local dealer and enjoy the thrill of a demonstration in the 1953 Jaguar
with automatic transmission. *Then you'll know that Jaguar is the one fine car for you.*

HOFFMAN MOTOR CAR CO., INC.
Importer East of the Mississippi
487 Park Avenue, New York

CHARLES H. HORNBURG, JR., INC.
Importer West of the Mississippi
9176 Sunset Blvd., Los Angeles

Guaranteed factory parts and complete service at dealers in most major cities

THE FINEST CAR OF ITS CLASS IN THE WORLD

XK-120 Sports Coupe,
sedan comfort with
racing car performance

XK-120, world's fastest
production car,
132.6 miles per hour

XK-120 Convertible,
handsomely appointed—120
miles per hour performance

2-251F

Chapter Three

The 1950s

After the less-than-successful first effort at Le Mans in 1950, Jaguar returned a year later with a new car. Labeled the XK120C (or C-type, the "C" was for Competition), the car was a sleek, lightweight, aerodynamic version of the road car. One writer called the C-type body "purposeful-looking and stark." The aluminum body was designed by Malcolm Sayer, who would go on to design other great Jaguar sports cars. The space frame chassis carried an uprated 220 horsepower version of the 3.4-liter XK engine. To reach this level, the compression ratio was raised to 9.0:1 and high-lift camshafts were fitted. A wide choice of gear and axle ratios was available. There was torsion-bar suspension front and rear. The C-type

1953 JAGUAR XK120M
The XK120M (the "M" was for Modified) had an improved 3.4-liter XK engine that delivered 190 horsepower, as opposed to the 160 horsepower of the original. The extra power came from race-bred high-lift camshafts and 8.0:1 compression ratio pistons.

won at Le Mans in 1951 at the record average of 93.5 miles per hour. The car driven by Peter Walker and Peter Whitehead led a team of three cars to overall victory, and the car driven by Stirling Moss and Jack Fairman was leading when the engine failed.

Later in the year, Moss repeated his Tourist Trophy win in Northern Ireland, this time driving a C-type, with Peter Walker finishing second. The car driven by Tony Rolt and Leslie Johnson finished third.

Jaguar expanded on the business side as well, buying the neighboring Daimler factory on Browns Lane, Coventry. Daimler was a company that had descended from the original Daimler company of Germany. While the German company was renamed Daimler-Benz after the 1926 merger of Daimler and Benz and eventually became Mercedes-Benz, the British company retained the Daimler name and regularly supplied limousines and sedans to the Royal Family. Jaguar's purchase of the

37

1953 JAGUAR C-TYPE
In 1951, Jaguar launched an assault on Le Mans with the XK120C, or C-type. The "C" was for Competition. The C-type was a pure racing car, with a space frame chassis made up of steel tubing and an independent rear suspension. The aerodynamic body, designed by Malcolm Sayer, was built of aluminum. Jaguar won the 1951 Le Mans 24 Hours with a C-type driven by Peter Walker and Peter Whitehead. When the 1952 cars retired due to overheating, the car was redesigned slightly for the 1953 race and was made 120 pounds lighter. This 1953 version represents the cars that finished first, second, fourth and ninth in the 1953 race.

factory and the name added significant prestige to the company.

In 1952, the merger of the British manufacturing companies Austin and Morris into the British Motor Corporation had little immediate impact on Jaguar, although BMC did build and distribute Austin-Healey sports cars, which were priced below the XK120.

Jaguar's 1952 Le Mans effort wasn't as successful as 1951, because a new streamlined body designed by Sayer developed cooling problems. All three works cars retired. Later in the year, Phil

JAGUAR XK120 FIXED HEAD COUPE
Jaguar's XK120 Fixed Head Coupe, introduced in 1951, had a remarkable resemblance to the Bugatti Atlantique coupe. Both had long hoods, sweeping fenders, "bullet" headlights, split windshields, and cramped cockpits. The similarities weren't accidental, because William Lyons was an acknowledged fan of the Bugatti and wanted his car to look like it. This XK120 is owned by Les Jackson.

Hill won one of his first races in a C-type sponsored by Jaguar West Coast distributor Charles Hornburg Jr.

The cooling problems were solved for the 1953 Le Mans race. Disc brakes were also added to the cars, which were 120 pounds lighter thanks to the use of lightweight electrical equipment and aircraft-style fuel tanks. With an even more powerful version of the 3.4-liter engine, (Weber carburetors replacing SUs) and a redesigned rear suspension that incorporated a Panhard rod and a torque arm, C-types finished first, second, fourth and ninth, led by the team of Tony Rolt and Duncan Hamilton.

Jaguar had introduced a Fixed Head Coupe (hard top) version of the XK120 in 1951. A Drop Head Coupe version followed in May 1953. The Drop Head was more closely related to an American convertible, with wind-up windows and more creature comforts than the original Open Roadster. The top could be raised and lowered in a matter of seconds, and its bracing structure was completely concealed by a padded and fully lined mohair top. Inside, the Drophead Coupe had a walnut-veneer dash and door trim as did the Fixed Head Coupe.

The Fixed Head Coupe bore a striking resemblance to the Bugatti Atlantique, with the long

JAGUAR XK120 FIXED HEAD COUPE AND XK8 CONVERTIBLE
Jaguar's first Fixed Head Coupe, the XK120, and its newest sports car, the XK8, sit side-by-side in an Alexandria, Virginia, courtyard, displaying the advances in automotive design in 50 years. The XK120 is a "vertical" design, while the XK8 is more "horizontal," showing more attention to aerodynamics. The XK120 is owned by Les Jackson.

hood, horseshoe-shaped grill and flowing hood and fenders. The resemblance is no coincidence. Lyons was an avowed fan of Bugatti designs. In fact, according to XK120 FHC owner Les Jackson, there are reports that when Lyons was informed that the seating capacity in the FHC was cramped, he said he didn't care as long as the Bugatti-like lines were retained.

Jackson also notes that "the design department apparently ran out of pencils when they got to the back of the car." Where the front two-thirds of the car is a pleasant combination of sweeping lines and compound curves, the rear is bland, and appears to have been copied from an Austin-Healey 100 or the yet-to-be-produced MGA.

Despite the use of disc brakes on the Le Mans winning C-type, the XK 120 and later 140 were still supplied with drum brakes. One other feature that indicated the direction the sedans would follow was the addition of a 3-speed automatic transmission for the Mark VII.

1954 JAGUAR XK140
When Jaguar began offering a Borg-Warner 3-speed automatic transmission in the XK140, it may have offended some sports car "purists," but the company was recognizing what modern producers of sport utility vehicles are realizing; not all vehicles are driven the way they are built to be driven. Many XK140 owners used their cars for sporty driving, rather than racing. They would appreciate the convenience of an automatic transmission, especially if they were driving in the Fixed Head Coupe, with its superior weather protection.

Now... the convenience of Borg-Warner
automatic transmission
available in the **Jaguar XK-140**
convertible and hardtop coupe.

1957 XK140
Successor to the XK120 was the XK140, introduced in 1954. The prime exterior difference between the XK120 and the XK140 was in the grille; the 140 had fewer vertical slats. The 140's bumpers were also heavier. With an engine that had been moved forward in the chassis by 3 inches, and additional modifications to the chassis, the seats were moved forward, which created more room in the car. The XK140 also benefited by the installation of the 190 horsepower version of the 3.4-liter XK engine. Power was raised to 210 horsepower by a Special Equipment, or SE, version that used C-type cylinder heads.

In October 1954, the XK120's successor, the XK140, was announced. The XK140 used rack-and-pinion steering, replacing the recirculating ball steering box of the XK120. The most distinguishing physical difference between the XK120 and XK140 was the latter car's new grille with fewer vertical bars and heavier front and rear bumpers. The XK140 also had greatly improved brakes but they were still drums. It soon became a familiar sight on highways and race tracks. Improvements were made in the engine compartment as well, with a new "C-type" cylinder head developing 210 horsepower from the 3.4-liter engine.

Also introduced at that London Motor Show was the Mark VII M sedan, with a 190 horsepower version of the 3.4-liter engine, a new front fascia with better headlights and driving lamps, and restyled bumpers.

The C-type was replaced as the factory race car by the D-type in 1954, also known as the XK120S Series 4. The D-type's Le Mans initiation wasn't quite as successful as the C-type's, though. It finished second in the 1954 race. A C-type finished fourth. But the D-type came back to win in 1955, 1956 and 1957, the last two years in Ecurie Ecosse-owned cars.

The 1955 cars were 7.5 inches longer than the 1954 cars and had a tonneau cover over the

1955 JAGUAR D-TYPE 3.8

Replacing the C-type as the company's racer was, the D-type. This car had monocoque construction, as opposed to the space-frame construction of the C-type, with a magnesium alloy tub. While the D-type finished second to a Ferrari in the 1954 Le Mans race, it was credited with winning the disastrous 1955 event, in which more than 80 people were killed. D-types repeated his success in 1956 and 1957, the latter race being under the colors of Ecurie Ecosse, a private racing team.

While the C-type was successful at Le Mans in its first effort, the D-type had no such luck. In 1954, it finished second to a 4.5-liter Ferrari. Success came in the tragic 1955 race, however, when the D-type won after Mercedes-Benz withdrew. Jaguar repeated its win in 1956 with a factory-back D-type and in 1957 with a private entry D-type.

"passenger" seat with a fin behind the driver's head. The cars used higher wraparound windshields and the exhaust exited out the rear. Six cars were built.

Unfortunately, Jaguar's 1955 win was tainted by the accident with Pierre Levegh's Mercedes-Benz 300SL that caromed off Lance Macklin's Austin-Healey and into the crowd, killing more than 80 people. A Mercedes was leading when the company withdrew from the race, handing it to Jaguar.

The D-type was even lighter and more potent (250 bhp) than the C and had an unorthodox frame built around a central welded fabrication. Forward of this center section was a sub-frame to support the engine and front suspension.

Jaguar announced in October 1956 that it was withdrawing from racing as a factory team, but would continue to support private entries.

At the 1955 London Motor Show in October, Jaguar introduced a compact sedan, the 2.4, with a 112 horsepower 2.4-liter version of the venerable XK 6-cylinder engine. With a price of £895 ($1,500) plus tax, the economical sedan offered speeds of over 100 miles per hour and seating for five people in a luxurious leather-lined interior with a walnut-veneer dash.

The year 1956 was important for Jaguar in other ways as well. In recognition of his vast contributions to the British automobile indus-try, as well as national pride in winning Le Mans with cars from his company, William Lyons became Sir William Lyons early in the year when he was Knighted by Queen Elizabeth II.

That same year, Jaguar introduced the Mark VIII sedan, which was more luxurious than the Mark VII which preceded it. The Mark VIII used walnut veneer throughout the passenger compartment, including two picnic tables for rear-seat passengers. In addition, the car had three cigar/cigarette lighters for smoking passengers, clocks for front and rear passengers, and a veneered magazine rack for rear seat passengers in cars with a bench front seat. Under the bonnet was the 210 horsepower version of the 3.4-liter XK engine.

the car...the Jaguar XK-140 hardtop coupe... about to depart from
the Plaza 'midst a modest cloud of admiring glances. For this version of the fabulous "XK"
(there are three models) is considered by automotive aesthetes to be one of the
all-time gems of motor car design. The XK-140 HARDTOP is particularly favored
by business and professional men who make a *pleasure* of the *necessity* of
driving. Cozy, comfortable, luxuriously appointed ... and, of course,
pure JAGUAR in performance. With additional rear seating accommodation,
priced at approximately $3,900.

For the traveler, may we suggest that you ask your dealer about the "Visit Europe Delivery Plan."
Jaguar Cars North American Corporation, 32 East 57th Street, N. Y. 22, N. Y.
(Importer east of the Mississippi)
Charles H. Hornburg Jr., Inc., 9176 Sunset Blvd., Los Angeles, Cal.
(Importer west of the Mississippi)

the Jaguar Mark VII

The stately four door MARK VII SEDAN represents a pinnacle of automotive craftsmanship. Among its many virtues is the ability to carry six people swiftly over great distances . . . in supreme luxury.

The MARK VII is at home on any road . . . in town or country. Throughout the world it is frequently seen proudly bearing license plates marked *Corps Diplomatique*.

The MARK VII is available with automatic transmission and standard equipment includes such amenities as a sliding sun roof, double fuel tanks to allow tremendous luggage capacity . . . lavish yet tasteful use of hand-rubbed walnut panelling and glove leather upholstery.

It is a car that gives its passengers as much pleasure as the owner behind the wheel.

SPECIFICATIONS

- **Engine:** Six cylinder 3½ litre twin overhead camshaft Jaguar XK engine developing 190 H.P. Twin S.U. horizontal carburetors.
- **Transmission:** Borg Warner automatic transmission. Four speed synchromesh gearbox with optional overdrive available on special order.
- **Suspension:** Independent front suspension; transverse wishbones, torsion bars and telescopic shock absorbers. Rear: Half elliptic springs controlled by telescopic shock absorbers.
- **Brakes:** Vacuum servo-assisted hydraulic. Friction lining area 179 sq. ins.
- **Steering:** Recirculating ball. Adjustable steering wheel.
- **Wheels:** Steel disc wheels with Dunlop 6.70 x 16 in. tubeless tires.
- **Fuel Supply:** Twin S.U. electric pumps. Capacity 20½ gallons in two tanks of 9½ and 11 gallons. Turn-over switch on instrument panel.
- **Electrical:** 12 volt 64 amp/hour battery.
- **Instruments:** 120 mph speedometer, tachometer, ammeter, oil pressure, water temperature and fuel gauges, electric clock.
- **Body:** Four door all steel six seater with sliding roof. Built-in heater, defroster and windshield washers. Upholstered in finest quality leather over foam rubber. Polished walnut panels.
- **Luggage Accommodations:** Capacious 17 cubic foot trunk with spare wheel fitted inside.
- **Dimensions:** Wheelbase 10 ft.; overall length 16 ft. 4½ ins.; width 6 ft. 1 in.; height 5 ft. 3 ins.; dry weight 3696 lbs.

1956 2.4, XK140, MARK VII

Jaguar's 1956 brochure showed the versatility of the company, with offerings of a compact sedan—the 2.4, a thoroughbred sports car—the XK140, and a large sedan—the Mark VII. The XK140 and Mark VII were powered by the 3.4-liter XK 6-cylinder engine, while the new 2.4 used a smaller version of the same engine. The 2.4 offered 30 miles per gallon and 100 miles per hour performance in a compact sedan that could comfortabley carry five passengers. The XK140 was the second-generation postwar Jaguar sports car, combining knowledge gained from the XK120 as well as three wins at the Le Mans 24 Hours race. The Mark VII was a full-size sedan with seating for six in "supreme luxury."

1956 XK140 FIXED HEAD COUPE

Jaguar's XK140 Fixed Head Coupe offered the ultimate for the "Man About Town." Here was a sports car of the highest magnitude, yet it was also a closed coupe that would protect the driver and his passenger from the elements. And a rear seat was available. The price was a reasonable $3,900.

1957 JAGUAR XKSS
When Jaguar withdrew from factory racing in 1956, it still had some spare D-type chassis lying around the factory. The solution was to take the cars, equip them with road gear to make them "street legal," and sell them as production cars. These cars were called the XKSS. Unfortunately, a fire in the Jaguar factory on February 12, 1957, wrote the final chapter on the XKSS shortly after the first one had been written. With only 16 cars completed, the remaining stock of XKSS chassis were destroyed in the fire, as well as several sedans. Jaguar returned to production within a week, but the XKSS was never revived.

With the end of factory-backed racing, there were a few D-type chassis lying around the factory. Lyons had an excellent idea what to do with them. The solution was to add bumpers, a muffler and top to the cars to make them suitable for road use and sell them to the public as the XKSS. With a list price in the United States of $5,600, it was expensive, but desirable. Unfortunately, a fire at the Browns Lane factory on February 12, 1957, destroyed most of the XKSS cars that were being built, leaving a production run of just 16. Limited production of regular cars returned to Browns Lane in just two days. Less than two weeks later, the company introduced the 3.4 sedan, which was a larger-engined version of the 2.4. Full production also returned to Browns Lane shortly, but without the XKSS.

The next version of the sports car was the XK150, which was introduced at the New York Auto Show in March 1958. The engine was the 210 horsepower version of the XK 3.4, but servo-assisted four-wheel disc brakes were now available for stopping. The transmission was a 4-speed manual, but a 3-speed automatic was available. An "S" version of the XK150 became available later, with a three-carburetor version of the 3.4-liter engine tuned to D-type specifications and developing 250 horsepower. This

1957 JAGUAR XK150
The XK150 was the ultimate expression of the XK line. While it was heavier and wider than the XK120 and 140, it had a curved one-piece windshield that improved the styling, and power options that helped the 3.8-liter XK engine develop as much as 265 horsepower to improve performance. The XK150 also had wind-up windows, which forced the elimination of the low-cut doors of the XK140.

With sedans as its bread-and-butter line, Jaguar sports cars have always played second fiddle. The problem for the ad people was how to turn this into an advantage. Make it exclusive! Only 7,500 XK150s would be sold in the United States, making it exclusive. And what a car it was. Four-wheel disc brakes, one-piece windshield, roll-up windows and a sensible convertible top made the XK150 as comfortable as any sedan, with a lot more performance than most sedans could offer.

car was only available with a manual transmission, however. All these had rack and pinion steering and disc brakes.

In October 1959, the new 3.8-liter XK engine became available for the XK150. In standard form, this engine developed 220 horsepower, but in "S" tune it pumped out 265 horses.

Along with the XK150, Jaguar also introduced its latest large "Saloon," the Mark IX in October 1958. Powered by the 3.8-liter XK 6-cylinder, and with standard disc brakes and power steering, the Mark IX was a true luxury sedan.

Jaguar introduced Mark 2 versions of the 2.4 and 3.4 sedans in 1959, along with a 3.8-liter version of the compact sedan, also designated Mark 2, even though there was no "Mark 1" 3.8. As they should have, the Mark 2 versions were improved versions of the original cars. Larger glass area gave the A-pillars a slimmer, more attractive line. A wider rear track, designed to improve handling, also eliminated the

Successor to the XK140 was the XK150 (left), with a slightly more bulbous body, but improved interior room. Introduced in 1957, it was built until 1961, by which time it had become the most prolific range ever built by Jaguar to that time. The cockpit was widened by 4 inches and a curved one-piece windshield was fitted in place of the flat two-piece affairs of the XK120 and 140. Top speed for the original XK150 was in excess of 135 miles per hour. In 1959 and afterward, the XK150 was powered by the 3.8-liter version of the XK engine. In standard form this engine developed 220 horsepower, while in "S" form, power was up to 265 horsepower. This XK150 is pictured next to an XKS.

"pinched in" look of the original cars. Up front, standard fog lights were fitted in place of the air intakes. The bigger 3.8-liter engine made the cars more competitive in touring car races and rallies. Automatic and manual gearboxes were offered.

Mark 2s had enviable racing records in British sedan racing, until Ford brought Galaxies over with big honking V-8 engines that Jaguar simply couldn't compete with. Among the drivers were Roy Salvadori, Graham Hill, Jack Sears, Colin Chapman and American Walt Hansgen. Jack Coombs prepared many Mark 2s for racing, including Hansgen's. He recalled Hansgen for this writer when we did an article on the Mark 2 for *Automobile Quarterly*:

"Walt Hansgen was the most exciting driver I have ever seen. I had him over here and he drove my Mark 2. He would go into Woodcote Corner [at Silverstone] absolutely sideways. I asked him what speed he was going and he said, 'John, it's a bit difficult to tell you. I haven't got time to look at the instruments. I'm a little busy.' But Walt was the best Mark 2 driver. He just chucked it sideways. He was a great character."

Jaguar closed out the 1950s in strong form, with a wide variety of cars to offer in a wide variety of classes, from sports cars to large sedan. The following decade, though, would see a period of turmoil for the company, both in the marketplace and in the corporate offices.

Jaguar

Versatile beauty. Responsive as a sports car yet meticulously fitted with all the appurtenances of supreme comfort. Tailored for family driving.

1959 JAGUAR 3.4 SEDAN

The 1959 Jaguar 3.4 Sedan offered everything a Jaguar owner would want in a compact sedan. For less than $4,600, a buyer could obtain performance of an XK150 (or at least the same engine and transmission of an XK150) with the traditional luxury of a Jaguar sedan, all in a compact package. There was no mistaking a Jaguar coming at you down the highway, either. With its oval grille and vertical chrome slats flanked by two huge headlights, there was nothing that looked quite like a Jaguar 3.4.

JAGUAR MARK IX SEDAN

Jaguar's Mark IX Saloon, or sedan, was introduced in October 1958, and would be the last "old style" sedan built by Jaguar. The next generation Mark X would be a longer, lower, more aerodynamic vehicle. The Mark IX, though, was a true large luxury sedan, with leather upholstery, walnut veneer dash and the powerful 3.8-liter XK double overhead cam 6-cylinder engine. The Mark IX also had power steering and front disc brakes for stopping. Skirts over the rear wheels aided aerodynamics slightly. As evidence of the market Jaguar was hoping to compete in with the Mark IX, compare this car with a Rolls-Royce of the era and note the strong similarities. The only major difference is in the grille. *Margaret Harrison*

TOP RIGHT
1961 JAGUAR XK150

The last year of production for the XK150 was 1961, when this car was built. The XK150 was available with the 3.8-liter engine that offered exhilarating performance. A choice of transmissions was also offered, with a four-speed manual (with or without overdrive) as standard and a Borg: Warner three-speed automatic as optional. Special Equipment XK150s were available with wire wheels, dual exhausts, fog lamps and windshield washers.

RIGHT
1960 JAGUAR MARK IX

The Jaguar Mark IX sedan showed little exterior change from the Mark VIII. Under the skin, however, there were several changes, prime of which was the installation of a 3.8-liter double overhead cam 6-cylinder engine rated at 225 horsepower. This was also the first Jaguar sedan to be offered with standard front disc brakes and power steering. The engine offered more power, the disc brakes offered the opportunity to stop the two-ton sedan more easily, and the power steering made it possible to handle it more easily.

The
1960s

Chapter Four

Jaguar had established its American ties early, beginning with Lyons' 1948 trip to the United States to set up sales and service agents. Lyons' relationship with importer Max Hoffman soured when Hoffman rejected Lyons advice and began importing Mercedes-Benz cars in 1953. That same year, Jaguar hired Johannes Eerdmans, to set up an import company in Manhattan.

In May 1960, Jaguar bought the Daimler factory at Radford in Coventry for £3.4 million, which became the main production center for engines and suspension units.

1963 JAGUAR E-TYPE

Few cars have had the impact on the world of automobiles as the Jaguar E-type, introduced in 1961. Its sleek aerodynamic lines were unlike anything seen on the road until that time. Designed by Malcolm Sayer, the E-type (or XKE in the United States) was powered by a 265 horsepower 3.8-liter XK engine at first that gave it a top speed in the neighborhood of 150 miles per hour. The E-type also had 4-wheel disc brakes, with the rear brakes mounted inboard.

Jaguar bought Coventry Climax in 1963, gaining an important engine developer. Some rumors said the only reason Lyons bought Coventry Climax was to regain the services of Walter Hassan, who had left Jaguar to work there. By 1965, Jaguar Cars Inc. had become the Jaguar Group, with 20 different companies under the corporate umbrella, including Daimler, Coventry Climax and Guy trucks.

In order to reduce his involvement with the company, Sir William named 16 "executive directors" in June 1966. One month later, Jaguar merged with the British Motor Corporation to form British Motor Holdings (BMH). The idea of the merger, at least in Jaguar's mind, was that BMC's size and assets would provide Jaguar with a sound financial and engineering base. While Sir William still remained in titular control of the company, corporate interests dictated many moves. Lyons relinquished the role of Managing Director to "Lofty" England early in 1968.

The gentlemen are discussing automotive performance. But, as Jaguar owners, they should know better than compare the speed of the new XK-E with that of the 3.8 Sedan, since speed alone has never been the criterion of excellence in judging Jaguars. How, then, you may ask, does one choose between the XK-E and the 3.8 Sedan? Both offer dramatic acceleration, phenomenal performance and superb handling. Therefore, let your own personal require-ments be the basis for your choice between the two. If there are two of you, then by all means investigate the new XK-E. But, if family needs dictate a roomier vehicle, then avail yourself of the comforts and spaciousness of the 3.8 Sedan. Both are, after all, thoroughbred Jaguars. For more information on both of these fine automobiles, consult your nearest Jaguar Dealer, or write JAGUAR CARS INC., 32 East 57th Street, New York 22, N. Y.

The Jaguar XK-E vs. the 3.8 Sedan

1961 XK-E AND 3.8 SEDAN
Both the XK-E (or E-type) and the 3.8 Sedan were powered by the venerable 3.8-liter XK 6-cylinder engine. By 1961, when this ad appeared, the engine was almost 15 years old. It would continue in operation into the 1980s. While the E-type offered stirring sports car performance, the 3.8 Sedan would take the same engine/transmission combination and put it in a compact five-passenger sedan. Nissan called its 1990s Maxima "the four-door sports car." It is a definition that Jaguar could have used 30 years earlier.

Unification of the British automobile industry continued in 1968 when BMH and Leyland Motor Corporation joined, forming British Leyland Motor Corporation. Sir William was named deputy chairman of BLMC under Lord Stokes. The new corporation joined 95 percent of the British-owned motor industry under one banner.

Johannes Eerdmans had been president of the successful Jaguar Cars North America since 1954. He held this position through the formation of British Leyland and retired in 1969. Graham Whitehead, as president of British Leyland Motors Inc., replaced him as Jaguar's U.S. chief.

On the automotive side, the 1960s were highlighted by the introduction and development of the E-type (or XKE in the United States). Rumors of a new and full-blooded Jaguar sports car grew through 1960. Introduced at the Geneva Salon in March 1961, the E-type was an instant success. Designed by Malcolm Sayer, it had some of the lines of the D-type and prototype E2A racer that followed it. But here was a completely new road car with a look unlike any other. The car was introduced in two forms—Open Roadster (or convertible) and Fixed Head Coupe. It was the latter, with its dramatic fastback styling and faired-in headlights, that the public fell in love with.

Powered by a 265 horsepower version of the XK 3.8-liter engine, the E-type had performance

1961 JAGUAR E-TYPE
Jaguar's E-type (or XK-E) hit the sports car world like an A-bomb. It offered stirring styling in both Coupe and Roadster forms, but it was the Coupe that elicited the most excitement. Fastback styling was still fairly new to most Americans, and when they saw the E-type, they went wild. The back door opened to reveal a healthy storage compartment, while the nose tipped forward to reveal the three-carburetor 3.8-liter XK 6-cylinder engine.

to match its good looks. The engine and gearbox were mounted in a detachable fabricated subframe with box-section frame members carrying the coachwork.

The coupe could go from 0-60 miles per hour in seven seconds and had a top speed of 151 miles per hour. It handled, too. The front suspension was by wishbones and torsion bars. Telescopic

Newest of Jaguars: The classic Mark X luxury sedan

As of today, the fine-car connoisseur has nothing left to wish for. Because here, with the introduction of the new Jaguar Mark X Sedan, is luxury rarely equalled; performance without peer. Under way, new monocoque construction and independent rear suspension afford a ride that is nothing short of phenomenal. Appointments are of the finest, and typically Jaguar. Seats are of the finest glove leather, with those in front fully reclining. Cabinet work is of hand-crafted walnut, mated and matched. Walnut tables, each with a vanity mirror, fold rearward from the front seat-backs. Standard equipment includes power-assisted steering, two independent brake systems (power-assisted), dual fuel pumps and lockable dual fuel tanks, automatic transmission with intermediate gear-hold for passing. Look for the Mark X at your Jaguar dealer's or write JAGUAR CARS INC., 32 East 57th St., N. Y. 22, N. Y. Jaguar Technical Service and Parts Headquarters, 42-50 Twenty-First Street, Long Island City 1, New York

1962 JAGUAR MARK X

The 1962 Mark X offered the consumer pure Jaguar luxury and performance at a reasonable price; reasonable when you compare it to a Rolls-Royce which offered slightly more luxury and less performance at a higher price. The Mark X Sedan offered leather seating ("glove soft"), hand-crafted walnut cabinetry, including walnut tables with vanity mirrors on the backs of the front seats, monocoque construction and a fully independent suspension.

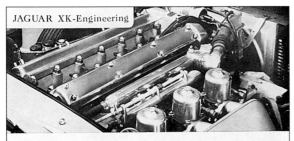

JAGUAR XK-Engineering

The Jaguar engine

To the untutored observer, the excitement that is the new Jaguar XK-E very likely begins and ends with a single glance at the long, lithe lines of this dramatic motor car. But the astute autophile realizes that total appreciation requires, among other things, an appraisal of the mighty heart that beats within the XK-E.

Upon opening the massive hood, dyed-in-the-wool Jaguar lovers will recognize an old friend. Modified, improved and increased slightly in capacity, it is still in essence the same thunderous, twin overhead-cam, six-cylinder power plant that has proved its reliability in winning hard-fought victories the world over and has made Jaguar famed and feared on every major racing circuit.

With a displacement of 230.6 cu. in. and a compression ratio of 9 to 1, the Jaguar XK-Engine develops 265 bhp at 5500 rpm, with torque an impressive 260 lbs. ft. at 4000 rpm. The cooling system features a fan which is thermostatically

controlled and operates independently of the engine, thereby eliminating fan drag at road speeds. For those interested in such figures, performance translates to 0-60 in 6.4 seconds, 0-100 in 16.0 seconds and time for the standing quarter-mile of 14.6 seconds. Of more importance to the average driver is the fact that, thanks to superior engineering, the XK-Engine may be driven in top gear at speeds of 10-15 mph without a trace of lugging or roughness.

It is important to note that in addition to the rigid inspection of all components during manufacture, each and every Jaguar XK-Engine is individually bench tested prior to installation—a procedure which ensures a performance and dependability second to none in the automotive field. We cordially invite you to view this, and the many other aspects of Jaguar XK-Engineering soon at your local dealer's and discover for yourself why Jaguars are the most advanced automobiles on the road. JAGUAR CARS INC., 32 East 57th St., New York 22, New York.

JAGUAR XK-Elegance

1962 JAGUAR E-TYPE

The essence of the Jaguar E-type was its three carburetor double overhead cam XK 6-cylinder engine. William Lyons always was concerned with the esthetics of his automobiles, whether from the outside or the inside. Consequently, his engines always dazzled the eye when you opened the hood. The 4.2-liter (230.6 cubic inch) engine developed 265 horsepower at 5,500 rpm, or 1.15 horsepower per cubic inch. And yet the XK-E was still elegant enough to accommodate a young lady in a fur coat.

shock absorbers were at all four corners. It is in the final abandonment of the conventional heavy rigid rear axle that this car broke most with Jaguar tradition. The rear suspension was mounted on a sub-frame and was by two pairs of coil springs with universal-jointed half-shafts located by radius arms and transverse links. Dunlop disc brakes were all around, with the rears mounted inboard.

At the time, the sports car market in the United States was a full one, with MGA, TR4, Austin-Healey 3000 and Alfa Romeo at the lower end and the Daimler SP250 somewhere in the middle. The E-type had a list price of $5,595 for the convertible and $5,895 for the coupe.

In the E-type's race debut, Graham Hill drove an Equipe Endeavour car to victory over Roy Salvadori in John Coombs' similar car at Oulton Park. It was the first of many wins for the sleek car.

The year 1961 was a watershed year on the sedan front as well. Jaguar introduced the Mark X in October at the London Motor Show. Here was a sleek modern sedan to replace the classic Mark IX, with a monocoque body that was longer and lower than its predecessors, but built on the same wheelbase. The Mark X used the 265 horsepower 3.8-liter XK engine and independent rear suspension of the E-type to record some impressive statistics for a big car; 0-60 miles per hour in under 11 seconds and a top speed of 115 miles per hour. A 4.2-liter version of the same engine powered the 1965 car, introduced in 1964. While this engine had the same nominal horsepower, a 10 percent increase in torque made it a better performer. Top speed was up to 122 miles per hour.

The same 4.2-liter engine made its debut in the 1965 E-type. Externally, the only distinction between the original cars and the 4.2 was a small badge on the trunk lid. Inside, there were new seats that were more comfortable and the elimi-

The sportscar.

Five minutes behind the wheel will tell you why the 1964 Jaguar XK-E is the new standard by which all sportscars are compared.

For one thing, it doesn't look like any other car you have ever seen. And it is capable of phenomenal speed and acceleration.

Yet its handling qualities give you the relaxed confidence of always being in complete command.

whatever the road, speed or driving conditions.

What's more, the 32 unique performance and luxury features of the XK-E are on each car when you buy it. With many other sports cars, they are added "extras."

A few of these features: the race-proven engine; "Monocoque" body; all-around independent suspension; four-wheel disc brakes;

bucket seats fully covered with genuine leather; completely instrumented dash panel.

See and drive the Jaguar XK-E. Roadster: $5,325 P.O.E. Coupe $200 more. (If you're going to Europe, inquire about Jaguar's money-saving Overseas Delivery Plan.) There are Jaguar dealers coast-to-coast. Jaguar Cars Inc., New York 22, N. Y.

The 1964 Jaguar XK-E

1964 JAGUAR E-TYPE
The 1964 Jaguar E-type (or XK-E) Coupe was priced at $5,525 in the United States. As such, it was probably one of the best values for the dollar. It offered the most aerodynamic body of its time, with wire wheels, leather seats, 4-wheel disc brakes, fully independent suspension and monocoque construction.

nation of brushed aluminum trim on the dash and transmission tunnel. Even with the automatic transmission installed after 1966, the E-type 4.2 would accelerate from 0-60 miles per hour in under 9 seconds and reach a top speed of over 136 miles per hour.

In October 1963, Jaguar introduced improved versions of the 3.4 and 3.8 Mark 2, calling them the 3.4S and 3.8S. These cars were 6 inches longer overall to accommodate the independent rear suspension. This extra length was used to good advantage by increasing the luggage capacity and providing for dual fuel tanks. Interior room improved as well, with the real benefit going to rear seat passengers.

Jaguar introduced yet another variation of the E-type, the 2+2 Coupe, in March 1966. Built on a chassis that was lengthened by 9 inches, the new car had rear seats that were usable by children or one adult on a long run. In addition, the roofline was raised 2 inches, which improved rear headroom. The extra 220 pounds of weight raised 0-60 miles per hour acceleration times to 8.3 seconds, though.

In a marriage between the large sedans and the compact versions, Jaguar introduced the 420 and 420G in October 1966. This car retained the general profile of the S-Class cars, but with a rectangular grille reminiscent of the Mark X. "Eyebrows" over the four headlights were another carryover from the S-type, although American versions had four equal-size headlights. In Europe the inner lights were smaller in diameter. The engine in the 420 was a two-carburetor version of the E-type's three-carburetor engine, delivering 245 horsepower.

While the 420 was derived from the S-Types, the 420G was clearly a derivative of the Mark X. The 420G had a wheelbase that was over a foot longer than the 420 (120 inches vs. 107.3 inches) and was 14.3 inches longer overall (202 inches vs. 187.7 inches). Walnut veneer was used on the dash, which was one of the last to feature toggle switches for controls. These "unsafe" switches would soon be replaced by the "safer" rocker switch variety. The chrome horn ring would also disappear shortly.

At the New York Auto Show in the spring of 1968, Jaguar displayed the Piranha, which was a Bertone-bodied E-type 2+2. The chassis was modified slightly to take D-type wide-rim wheels and wider tires. After appearing at the show and another in Montreal, the car was auctioned by Parke-Bernet

1965 JAGUAR E-TYPE

By 1965, when this E-type was built, the engine capacity had been increased to 4.2 liters, although power was still 265 horsepower. Engine capacity was increased by increasing the bore by 5 mm. A new block was thus needed, which also required a new crankshaft. Jaguar used the cylinder head from the 3.8-liter engine, which did not match exactly with that of the 4.2. Inside, the only difference between this car and the original were new, more comfortable seats and the elimination of the polished aluminum trim around the dash and transmission tunnel.

1967 JAGUAR 3.4 SEDAN

While Jaguar had always built large sedans, the 2.4 and 3.4 (and later 3.8) were the company's first "mid-size" sedans. The first sedans were introduced in 1957, with "Mark 2" versions introduced two years later. The Mark 2 cars offered better visibility with more glass and thinner A-pillars. The 3.4-liter inline six engine developed 210 horsepower, giving it one horsepower per cubic inch displacement. The Mark 2 3.4 was then one of the world's first muscle cars. Wire wheels were offered as a factory option.

1966 JAGUAR E-TYPE

By 1966, when this Series III Jaguar E-type was built, federal regulations had eliminated the faring over the headlights and created a "chromier" grille. The car still retained its aerodynamic lines, although a more vertical windshield detracted somewhat from this. In order to overcome this loss of aerodynamics, the Series III cars were equipped with a 5.3-liter V-12 engine, the first production V-12 to appear since the Cadillacs of the 1930s. The engine was rated at 250 horsepower in the United States, and could be mated to a 4-speed manual or 3-speed automatic transmission.

Galleries. It brought $16,000 at a time when Jaguars were selling for $5,500 to $6,500.

While the large 420G remained in production, all the other Jaguar sedans were made obsolete with the introduction of the XJ6 in September 1968. Through the 1960s, Jaguar was building two completely different lines of sedans in addition to a range of three sports cars. This created a terrific strain on the company's resources. The solution was the XJ6, a mid-size sedan that replaced both existing sedan lines. It was a hit from the start. Here was a car that looked like the 420, but was sleeker and moved Jaguar in a new direction. With the traditional "Jaguar look," it was both trim and modern. While not as big as the Mark X, it was comfortable enough for five adults and offered infinitely better handling

and overall performance. Before the XJ6, Jaguar was a producer of sports cars and high performance sedans; after the XJ6 it was a producer of luxury cars.

Powered by the 4.2-liter XK engine that delivered 245 horsepower, the XJ6 made its mark by having low levels of noise, vibration and harshness years before "NVH" became a watchword for car engineers. Adding to the package were low-profile radial tires, which, with the independent front and rear suspensions mounted on sub-frames, added to the car's road silence. The dash featured burl walnut trim, eight round instruments and an imposing array of ten toggle switches splayed across the bottom of the dash.

Economy versions of the S-Type—the 240 and 340—were introduced in October 1967. While they retained the basic styling of the Mark 2 sedans,

1967 JAGUAR 340
In 1967, Jaguar introduced "economy" versions of the Mark II sedans, dubbed 240 and 340. This 340 was powered by the venerable 3.4-liter dohc XK six. While the exterior "bathtub" lines of the 340 were almost identical to those of its predecessors, economy was introduced with Ambla vinyl, rather than leather, upholstery. The bumpers were single chrome bars rather than the double bars of the Mark II sedans, and wire wheels were no longer available. The owner of this 340 is Jim Spooner.

the 240 and 340 were truly low-price versions of a medium-priced car. For example, while the 2.4 and 3.4 had leather upholstery, the newer cars were trimmed in Ambla vinyl. The bumpers were slimmer single chrome bars, as opposed to the double bars of the Mark 2. And wire wheels were not available; steel discs were the order of the day. The 240 did get a power boost, though, from 122 horsepower of the original version to 133 in the 240.

Late in 1968, Jaguar introduced the Series II E-type, with modifications made necessary by U.S. Federal Safety regulations. The glass fairings on the headlights were removed in 1967 and the toggle switches replaced by rockers. For the Series II, the headlights were moved forward and the bumpers made more sturdy. A connection with history disappeared when the ears had to be removed from the wire wheel knock-offs, again as a safety measure. Clean air regulations dictated a replacement of the S.U. carburetors with Zenith-Strombergs, which

were cleaner. Thus restricted, the engine now delivered 246 horsepower vs. 265 in the "SU" version.

In the United States, Jaguar headquarters were located on the 12th floor of 32 East 57th Street, New York, where they had been since the late 1950s. Graham Whitehead was named president of Jaguar's U.S. operations in October 1968. Jaguar moved its headquarters to the British Leyland offices to Leonia, New Jersey. Jaguar would retain the location after the dissolution of British Leyland in the 1970s.

Briggs Cunningham had persuaded Jaguar to sell him the E2A prototype car, which was an evolutionary step between the D-type and E-type. Cunningham raced the car at Le Mans with no success, then brought it back to the United States. Painted in Cunningham's white-with-blue-stripes racing colors, it won at Bridgehampton with Walt Hansgen at the wheel. Cunningham then retired the car to his collection in California and sold it to the Collier Museum in Naples, Florida, in 1988.

Jaguar compact sedans, from the 3.4 through the 3.4 Mark II to the final iteration of the 340, were powered by the 3.4-liter dohc XK six. By the time the engine was installed in the 1967 340, it was more than 20 years old, but it had only reached middle age. The engine would continue to power Jaguars into the 1980s, although enlarged ultimately to 4.2 liters capacity. Crammed in the 340, though, it was a service nightmare even in an era of minimal additions for air conditioning and emissions controls.

The 340 was conceived and delivered as an "economy" version of the 3.4 Mark II compact sedan. These economies reached inside the car in the form of vinyl upholstery rather than the original leather and thinner padding in the seats. The burl walnut veneer dash, however, was retained from the Mark II sedans, as were the traditional round, white-on-black instruments. From the left, the instruments are speedometer, tachometer, water temperature, oil pressure, fuel level and battery amperage. Beneath the dash was a small tray that was useful for carrying maps.

With a rear end similar to the Mark I sedans, the only difference exhibited with the 340 was a thinner chrome bumper and chrome farings around the taillights. Even with the smooth rear end that has none of the aerodynamics of modern sports sedans, the Mark IIs and 340s were potent racing cars at the hand of such luminaries as Graham Hill and Roy Salvadori.

Chapter Five

The 1970s

The decade of the 1970s would see Jaguar, and all manufacturers, forced to deal with ever more stringent U.S. Federal safety and emissions legislation. These regulations would cripple engine performance until designers learned how to cope by offering more efficient fuel injection systems. In addition, styling would suffer to some degree with the addition of stronger bumpers and minimum headlight heights.

Jaguar had responded to these rules in the 1960s by modifying the E-type's headlights, for

1978 JAGUAR XJ6
While Jaguar has been revered and respected as a producer of high-performance sports cars, it is the Jaguar sedans that have been the bread-and-butter cars. Jaguar introduced the XJ6 in 1968, which was a successful marriage between the compact Mark 2 range and the larger 420 sedans. Powered by a 4.2-liter XK 6-cylinder engine, the XJ6 packaged traditional Jaguar values in a sedan that was years ahead of its time. Five people could ride in comfort in the XJ6, which used the same subframe-mounted rear suspension of the E-type, as well as the E-type's inboard rear disc brakes.

example, in the Series II cars. As that decade ended the glass headlight fairings had disappeared and more substantial bumpers changed the front fascia.

To improve the power situation, Jaguar introduced the Series III E-type in March 1971 with the first V-12 engine in series production since the Lincolns of the 1940s. The 5.3-liter V-12 in the E-type delivered 272 horsepower in Europe and 250 in the U.S. The introduction of the V-12 also meant universal use of the 9 inch-longer "2+2" wheelbase on all models.

The V-12 engine was based on a 5.0-liter concept used in the XJ13 racing prototype. The production version was an all-aluminum 5.3-liter engine with single overhead cams on each bank of cylinders. It was capable of propelling the E-type to 100 miles per hour in 15.5 seconds. Automotive writers all over the world have called the Jaguar V-12 "one of the world's great engines." In fact, its existence was denied for years by Jaguar until it was eventually restored after a

1971 JAGUAR E-TYPE V-12

The ultimate expression of the E-type was the 1971 Series III with the 5.3-liter V-12 engine. Some writers said the trend toward a heavier car with the aerodynamic concessions brought about by federal regulations reduced the sportiness of the E-type. Still, it was the only serious production vehicle with a V-12 engine and it still had the E-type panache. A Series III Roadster tested by *Road & Track* achieved a top speed of 135 miles per hour and went from 0-60 miles per hour in 7.4 seconds. What offended the purists, though, was the availability of a 3-speed Borg-Warner automatic transmission as well as a 4-speed manual gearbox.

crash during testing. The crash scotched any racing plans for it.

The engine had more than adequate power for the job and was smooth to boot. Power was listed as 272 horsepower vs. 265 for the latest 4.2-liter XK six. Two comparison tests by *Road & Track* show the performance difference. In 1969, *R&T* tested an XKE 2+2 with the 4.2-liter six and hit a top speed of 119 miles per hour and 0-60 miles per hour in 8.0 seconds. When the magazine tested a Series III Roadster with the V-12, the top speed was 135 miles per hour and the 0-60 time had dropped to 7.4 seconds. And the roadster was 300 pounds heavier than the 6-cylinder 2+2.

The V-12 had first seen the light of day in the XJ13 prototype. This mid-engined car had a four-cam version of the engine (production V-12s would have one cam per bank). With a possible goal as a future Le Mans competitor, the XJ13 was extensively tested.

As installed in the Series III E-type, the V-12 had a bore and stroke of 90 x 70 mm for a capacity of 5,343 cc. There was one chain-driven camshaft per bank of cylinders. The block and crankcase was aluminum. Cooling was by two electric fans. Fuel injection was tried, but the initial versions of the engine used four downdraft Zenith-Stromberg carburetors.

1971 SERIES III JAGUAR E-TYPE V-12

Putting a V-12 engine in the E-type made it a whole new kind of cat. True, the windshield wasn't as sharply raked as in the Series I E-type, and the mouth now had a proper grille and bumper overriders to protect it, but the presence of the first V-12 engine since the 1930s was more than enough to offset exterior physical deformities. The 5.3-liter engine developed 314 horsepower, or almost one horsepower for each of its 326 cubic inches. This "ultimate cat" also had 4-wheel disc brakes, a fully independent suspension and power-assisted rack-and-pinion steering for better control.

On the styling side, the Series III E-type had a grille of horizontal chrome strips over a larger air intake, necessitated by the V-12 installation, and bumper overriders to protect it. More significantly, a more vertical windshield detracted from the cleaner lines of the original E-type.

Sir William Lyons retired from Jaguar on March 3, 1972, ending a 50-year association with the

1966 JAGUAR XJ13 CONCEPT CAR
Even when Jaguar withdrew its backing from an official factory racing team, there had been discussions about the development of a V-12 engine. The test bed for that engine became the XJ13 concept car of 1966. XJ13 was designed by Malcolm Sayer and was a mid-engine configuration with a similarity to the E-type and other sports-racing cars of the era such as the Lola/Ford GT40 and McLaren-Elva. The car's existence was denied by Jaguar for many years, until it was time for the announcement of the production V-12. Unfortunately, XJ13 crashed during the filming of a commercial and was badly damaged. It was rebuilt in 1972 and began making public appearances in 1973.

company he founded. At his retirement he said he still believed that "motoring should be a joy and not a choice." Sir William was now 70 and reluctantly left his company in younger hands. Those hands belonged to F. R. W. "Lofty" England, who was 60 and had joined the company in 1946 as service manager. He was responsible for much of Jaguar's success at Le Mans. England's reign was a short one, however, as he was replaced in September 1973 by 34-year-old Geoffrey Robinson, appointed by the British Leyland board. Lofty England retired in 1974.

England was met with a strike when he first took office. The strike was caused by a change by the BL management of the way workers were paid. In the past, Jaguar workers were paid on a piece-work basis, where they were paid for the amount of work they did. BL changed that system to a day-rate payment basis. This was anathema to the way Jaguar had done business in the past and a 11-week strike crippled the company.

In July 1972, the V-12 engine became available in the XJ6 sedan, creating the XJ12. With a 241 horsepower (U.S. specs) engine lurking beneath the hood, the XJ12 was capable of a top speed of almost 140 miles per hour. The XJ12 also was equipped with power-assisted 4-wheel disc brakes, with the front brakes ventilated and

1973 JAGUAR V-12
The Series II E-types lost some of their aerodynamic penetration to a more vertical windshield and uncovered headlights. But still they were unmatched by any other cars on the road at the time. With the 5.3-liter V-12 engine under the hood, the E-type could accelerate from 0-60 miles per hour in 6.8 seconds and reach a top speed that was illegal in any state in the union. But with the smoothness of the V-12, you could also cruise at 10 miles per hour in top gear and accelerate to cruising speed.

1976 JAGUAR XJC COUPE
When Jaguar introduced the Series II XJ sedans, the company also introduced coupe versions in both six and V-12-engined versions. The cars were introduced in 1973, but weren't available until 1974. The reason for the delay was that the pillarless door design did not seal perfectly at high speed. By 1976, the Coupes also had to compete with the new XJS. Add to this the fact that the Coupes cost $750 more than the Sedans, and sales weren't what was expected.

the rear brakes mounted inboard, as in the E-Type, to reduce unsprung weight. Long wheelbase versions of both the XJ6 and XJ12 were introduced just two months later. These cars offered an extra 4 inches in wheelbase and 2 inches in overall length to improve rear seat leg room. With a 4-inch longer rear door, entry and exit also became easier.

Series II versions of Jaguar's entire XJ sedan line were introduced in September 1973. These redesigns were required to satisfy U.S. safety regulations which dictated a front bumper height of 16 inches. Since this would have put the bumpers in the middle of the XJ grille, the front end was redesigned. And as some reporters of the scene noted, the change lightened the look of the Jaguar

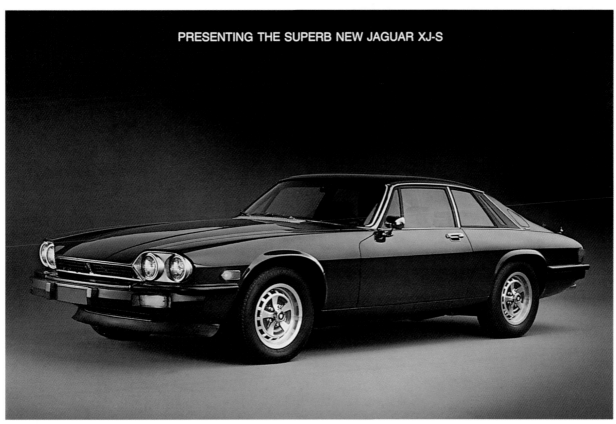

PRESENTING THE SUPERB NEW JAGUAR XJ-S

1976 XJS
Jaguar introduced the XJS in 1976, saying it had "the performance and handling of the more expensive sports cars and the quietness and comfort of luxury sedans." Maybe it was the quietness and comfort that made purists dislike the XJS. However, it was powered by the same 5.3-liter V-12 that had powered the E-type. Standard equipment included an 8-track AM/FM stereo sound system and a heated rear window.

front end, while similar changes to cars including the MGB and Triumph Spitfire served to destroy the looks of the cars.

The dash of the Series II XJ was also redesigned to replace the confusing, if handsome, array of rocker switches in front of the driver with a more logical arrangement. Instruments were now clustered in front of the driver in a redesigned instrument panel.

Two-door versions of the XJ sedans—XJ6C and XJ12C—were introduced along with the

Series II sedans. Due to a combination of problems, these cars did not sell well and were discontinued in 1975. With their windows down, these 2-door "hardtop" coupes looked like convertibles with their tops raised. This look was enhanced by the standard vinyl top of the coupes.

One of the reasons for dropping the XJ coupes was the introduction of the XJ-S sports coupe in September 1975. Initially shown at the Frankfurt Auto Show with a V-12 engine, the XJ-S was the last product to show the design hands of Sir

1977 JAGUAR XJS
By 1975, the E-type had been around for almost 15 years and was getting stale. Jaguar needed a new sports car to replace it, but the era of sports cars was also getting stale. The car that replaced the E-type was the XJS, which was introduced in September 1975. Powered by a 5.3-liter V-12 engine, the XJS was a 2+2 coupe with controversial "flying buttresses" around the rear window. While its styling was not universally admired, the XJS would survive for over 20 years and become the most-produced Jaguar sports car of all time.

William Lyons and Malcolm Sayer, who had died in 1970. This sports coupe filled the hole vacated by the E-type, which was discontinued in February 1975. But it was not a sports car in the sense the E-type coupes were. Rather, the XJ-S was more of a grand touring coupe in execution and use, although performance versions of the car did have some racing successes in the United States and Europe.

In true sports car tradition, though, the original XJ-S had a plain interior with leather upholstery. The car would remain essentially unchanged until 1982,

SIR WILLIAM LYONS (LEFT) AND SIR JOHN EGAN (RIGHT)
John Egan took over the reins of Jaguar in 1980, when Sir Michael Edwardes was appointed chairman of British Leyland. Sir William Lyons had an opportunity to meet Egan shortly after the latter took over. Egan was knighted in 1986 for his efforts in resuscitating Jaguar and saving it from the liquidators.

1978 XJ12
The most elegant Jaguar sedan was the XJ12, with the 5.3-liter V-12 engine, 3-speed GM automatic transmission, 4-wheel disc brakes, independent suspension all around, and such traditional Jaguar touches as walnut interior trim, leather seats and power-assisted rack-and-pinion steering. Dual fuel tanks made every trip to the gas station a thrill for the attendant, as did oil changes with the gleaming chrome head covers on the V-12 engine.

tion operating, which meant that the NEB had a major voice in day-to-day operations. Geoffrey Robinson resigned as managing director of Jaguar. Lord Ryder left the NEB in 1977, but the damage had been done. Michael Edwardes was named to head British Leyland (BL) in 1977 with a brief to restore it to profitability by virtually any means. A BL operations committee ran Jaguar until Bob Knight was named managing director in 1979. John Egan was hired as managing director by Michael Edwardes in 1980 and Knight retired at that time.

The Ryder Report's misguided attempt to centralize design, engineering and management functions by British Leyland nearly destroyed the spirit that existed in the individual car companies. At Jaguar, a core of people, primarily in engineering, kept the spirit of the company alive as well as the future model program.

when a High Efficiency version appeared. There were complaints about the styling of the XJ-S. which featured "buttresses" around the rear windows that limited rearward vision somewhat.

Powered by a 5.3-liter V-12 engine rated at 244 horsepower, the XJ-S had a top speed of over 135 miles per hour and looked as if it was going that speed even when standing still. One of the reasons for this was a unique styling feature of "flying buttresses" that swept from the roofline to the tail of the car. While these controversial buttresses aided the stability of the XJ-S at speed, they did reduce rearward vision.

Earlier in 1975, a British government report by the National Enterprise Board (NEB), named after its author, Lord Ryder, proposed uniting all British Leyland car manufacturing under one umbrella group, BL Cars. Government funding had to be provided to keep the crippled corpora-

GROUP 44 V-12 E-TYPE AT ROAD ATLANTA
Jaguar's return to racing in the United States was under the banner of Bob Tullius' Group 44 on the East Coast and Joe Huffaker on the West Coast. The Tullius effort was the more successful. Tullius first raced a V-12-engined E-type and was successful in his second year out, winning an SCCA National Championship.

Tullius went to a highly modified XJS after the E-type and won the SCCA's Trans-American Sedan Championship. All Group 44 cars were noted for their pristine finish. With Quaker State as a prime sponsor besides British Leyland, the cars were painted white with two shades of green as a bottom color.

Bob Knight, among others, fought to keep Jaguar engineering dedicated to Jaguar, rather than part of a corporate homogenization. While this ran counter to the aims of the Ryder Report, it was successful and Jaguar engineering remained independent. One of their tactics was to design the engine bay of the forthcoming XJ40 sedan so that it was too narrow to accommodate a Rover V-8, as BL wanted, and they would have to use a Jaguar straight six. Of course, when Jaguar eventually decided to add a V-12 to the line, this plan backfired.

On the competition front, Jaguar Cars Inc. in the United States supported two racing efforts, one under the tutelage of Bob Tullius' Group 44 on the East Coast and the other under Joe Huffaker on the West Coast. Tullius and Lee Mueller in the Huffaker car both drove E-types, with Tul-

1979 XJ6/12, XKS (S-TYPE)

By 1979, Jaguar was calling the XKS the "S-type" in an attempt to place it in the lineage of the C-type, D-type and E-type. The XKS wasn't a sports car in the classic sense; it had far more refinement and probably as good performance as most sports cars. The XKS used the 5.3-liter V-12 engine, which was enough to give it a certain panache. That engine was also available in the Jaguar Sedan, be it XJ6 or XJ12. In these two cars, Jaguar offered stirring performance and unmatched luxury.

lius' overall effort being the more successful. He finished second in the SCCA runoffs at Road Atlanta that year.

Tullius won the SCCA championship in 1975, competing against the likes of Corvette. He switched to an XJ-S in 1976 and won the SCCA's Trans-Am Sedan Championship in 1977 and

1979 JAGUAR XJ-S

"The most extravagant Jaguar ever built" was the elegant 1979 XJ-S. This was the street version of the car that, in Bob Tullius' hands, won five Trans-Am races in its first season. Yet here was also a four-passenger car with fully independent suspension, 4-wheel disc brakes, power rack-and-pinion steering and Jaguar's 5.3-liter V-12 engine.

1978. In the latter year he won seven of ten races. Tullius' final Trans-Am effort was in 1981 when he finished second, but by then the company's efforts were trending toward sports racing cars.

Another competition effort gave Jaguar a record that is likely to stand forever. It was in the 1979 Cannonball Baker Sea-to-Shining-Sea Memorial Trophy Dash from Darien, Connecticut, to Los Angeles. Begun by *Car and Driver* Editor Brock Yates early in the decade, it was both a tribute to the erstwhile Cannonball Baker, who set coast-to-coast records in the early years of the century in a variety of cars from Stutz to Cadillac, and it was also a challenge to the national 55 miles per hour speed limit. Yates and a group of competitors would try to be the first to reach Los Angeles.

In the fifth running of the event in 1979, Jaguar dealers Dave Yarborough and Dave Heinz ran the Cannonball in an XJ-S V12 coupe. They covered the 3,000-mile distance in 32 hours, 51 minutes, for an average speed of 86.7 miles per hour. Since it was also the last running of the Cannonball, Heinz' and Yarborough's record will stand forever.

Jaguar closed out the decade of the 1970s with the introduction of Series III versions of the XJ sedan range. With a new roofline and rear window to improve rear seat headroom, the Series III cars showed subtle styling changes which served to perfect the XJ design. Besides the roofline, the side windows slanted in slightly to a narrower roof, the windshield was slanted more sharply, and the wing windows were eliminated. Up front, the horizontal chrome bars of the grille were replaced by vertical bars, which continue to the 1997 models.

In Europe, the new XJ-S became available in 1984 with a choice of engines: a new 3.6-liter six, or the 5.3-liter V-12. In the U.S., however, only the V-12 was offered. Initially rated at 289 horsepower, power output grew to 295 horsepower in 1981. When fuel consumption concerns threatened to kill the V-12, the "Fireball" cylinder head of Swiss engineer Michael May was incorporated into the 1982 "HE" or High Efficiency versions of the engine.

The 1980s

Chapter Six

The 1980s began with Jaguar doing business as usual; moving through a period of rediscovered independence; and ending dramatically with the company under control of Ford and producing the fastest production car of the time. Jaguar returned to the scene of its greatest triumphs at Le Mans and took the prize home twice. On the sad side, founder Sir William Lyons died in February 1985.

Administratively, Jaguar Cars Ltd. ended its unhappy alliance with British Leyland by going public on June 29, 1984. Hamish Orr-Ewing was named chairman of the company, only to be ousted in 1985. John Egan continued through the decade as managing director, retiring in 1990.

1980 JAGUAR XJS
While Jaguar sales were suffering under the confused management of British Leyland in the early 1980s, the XJS continued to carry the banner of Jaguar sports cars. Bob Tullius campaigned an XJS to win the 1978 SCCA Trans-Am Sedan Championship in the V-12-engined car. A 6-cylinder version of the XJS was to come in 1985, but this 1980 car still used the elegant 5.3-liter V-12.

Jaguar production increased from 14,000 at the beginning of the decade to more than 50,000 in 1988, before the U.S. stock market crash of October 1987 put a crimp in all luxury car sales. American sales reached a peak of 24,464 in 1986

In 1984, 178 million Jaguar shares were offered on the British stock market for the first time, with the exception of a "Golden Share" held by the British government to protect the company from a takeover. The offering caused a rush on the London Exchange on August 3, 1984, when there were offers for eight times as many shares as were available. The price of the shares went to £1.88 ($2.94) within a week. In the United States, the over-the-counter price rose to $9.50 in early 1987.

A takeover at the time seemed unlikely. Profits rose to £120.8 million ($189 million) in 1986 and continued near the £100 million ($150 million) mark for several years. A new Engineering Centre was opened at Whitley, Coventry, in 1988. Jaguar Cars Inc., moved to new headquarters in the United States in June

79

1989 JAGUAR VANDEN PLAS MAJESTIC
Along with the introduction of the new AJ6 engine, Jaguar also introduced the Majestic version of the XJ6 Vanden Plas sedan in 1989. The Majestic only came in Regency Red and included a magnolia leather interior, alarm system and diamond-polished alloy wheels. It also included all the standard Vanden Plas features, such as a limited-slip differential, self-leveling suspension, and folding burl walnut picnic tables on the backs of the front seats.

1990. The new home office was located in Mahwah, New Jersey, in the north-central area of the state, near the New York border.

But all was not completely well. Profits dipped to £47.5 million ($74 million) in 1988, and £1.4 million in the first six months of 1989. In 1989, new competitors appeared from the Far East in the form of luxury cars introduced by the three major Japanese auto manufacturers: Honda's Acura, Toyota's Lexus and Nissan's Infiniti divisions.

John Egan realized that he no longer had the resources to fund product development on his own. Late in 1988, Egan met with Donald Petersen of Ford. Discussions broke off when it was apparent that Ford wanted a majority interest in Jaguar. Egan next went to General Motors. These discussions were more fruitful and GM agreed to an arrangement whereby it would buy 30 percent of Jaguar, but would leave the company independent.

After the brief courtship between Jaguar and GM during 1988, Ford came back into the picture and announced on September 19, 1989, that it would buy 15 percent of Jaguar's stock. Under American regulations and Jaguar articles of incorporation, this was the limit. Such a move also had to be made public. Three weeks later, GM made the same announcement. All this speculation fueled interest in Jaguar shares on the stock market, raising the price from around $5 to around $13.

FASTMASTERS JAGUAR XJ220
While the XJ220 didn't make it to production, approximately a dozen of these cars were used for a one-year racing series called FastMasters. Retired drivers such as Bobby Allison, Parnelli Jones and Jack Brabham raced in events that were companion races to NASCAR or CART events. The series proved to be popular and had TV sponsorship, but the costs of maintaining the cars far exceeded the public relations value.

On October 31, 1989, the British government withdrew its "Golden Share," permitting full takeover of Jaguar. GM had only wanted a minority interest in Jaguar; Ford had decided it wanted the whole package. Ford's offer was now the only acceptable one. On November 2, 1989, Ford purchased Jaguar for £8.50 ($13.28) per share or $2.5 billion (£1.6 billion). The transaction became official on January 1, 1990, when Jaguar Cars Ltd. became a wholly owned subsidiary of the Ford Motor Company.

John Egan told employees of Jaguar North America, "In 1980 when I became chairman of Jaguar, the company was worth nothing. It was a case of revive Jaguar or close it. In 1984, after four years of sales growth worldwide, when we floated our shares, the new worth was approximately $500 million. That in itself was not a bad turnaround. Now in 1989, the Jaguar board has approved an offer from Ford Motor Company of approximately two and one half billion dollars for Jaguar. That represents a five-fold increase in value since 1984."

Jaguar supported two competition efforts through the early years of the decade, but ended the decade backing just one team worldwide. Bob Tullius and Group 44 continued to be the corporate standard-bearer in the United States. After winning SCCA National Championships in the V-12-powered E-type and two Trans-Am Sedan Championships in the XJS, in 1982 Tullius received permission from Mike Dale of Jaguar Cars to build a prototype racer to compete in the International Motor Sports Association's GTP series in the United States. The car was the XJR-5 (XJ for experimental Jaguar, R for racer, 5 because it was the fifth Jaguar racer for Tullius). The body was designed by Len Dykstra, while the V-12 engine was derived from the 5.4-liter unit used in the XJ-S. In developed 525 horsepower. It its first race, the XJR-5 finished third at Road America. Its first win came in 1983 at Road Atlantic.

1988 LE MANS 24-HOUR VICTORY
Jaguar returned to the Le Mans winner's circle in 1988 with a three-car team of Tom Walkinshaw Racing cars sponsored by Silk Cut and Castrol. The winning car was driven by Johnny Dumfries, Jan Lammers and Andy Wallace, and the three remaining Jaguar cars in the race crossed the finish line after 24 hours in formation.

In Europe, Jaguar support went to Tom Walkinshaw Racing. Walkinshaw raced an XJ-S in the European Touring Car championship and won the title in 1984. Although Tullius spearheaded Jaguar's return to Le Mans in 1985 with a 13th place finish, it was TWR which would be competing in the World Sportscar Championship, which included Le Mans. An XJR-5 was shipped to TWR for analysis, but Walkinshaw had already commissioned a new design from Tony Southgate. Christened XJR-6, the car finished third in its first race at Mosport. Its first win was at Silverstone in May 1986. Group 44 and TWR would continue to build XJR racers, with Group 44 getting the odd numbers and TWR the even numbers.

Group 44 debuted its new car, XJR-7, at Daytona in 1985, where it finished fourth. Tullius and Chip Robinson won the December Daytona three-hour race that year, however. They won two more races in 1987, after it was announced that TWR would also campaign for Jaguar in the United States in 1988. The final race for Group 44 was at Watkins Glen, where there was an emotional "good-bye party" after the race.

For TWR, the 1987 car was the XJR-8, with a 7-liter V-12. The car won eight of ten world championship races and the World Championship of Sports Cars. In 1988 TWR won the Daytona 24 hours and brought Jaguar back to the winners' podium at Le Mans, after 31 years. The driving team of Johnny Dumfries, Jan Lammers and Andy Wallace was successful for Jaguar and TWR.

In February 1990, a TWR XJR-12 won the 24 Hours of Daytona in its first race, driven by Lammers, Andy Wallace and Davy Jones. Jaguar repeated its Le Mans win in 1990 in a car driven by John Nielson, Price Cobb and Martin Brundle. Lammers, Wallace and Franz Konrad finished second in another XJR-12.

In production cars, Jaguar developed a new 3.6-liter 6-cylinder engine that debuted in September 1983. Dubbed the AJ6 (for Advanced Jaguar), this engine would be used initially in the sport coupes, but would later also be used in sedans.

With a capacity of 3,592cc and dual overhead camshafts, the AJ6 was only slightly larger than the XK engine developed during World War II that had been so instrumental in Jaguar's resurgence. Compression ratio for the AJ6 was 9.6:1 and it developed 221 horsepower at 5,000 rpm initially with four valves per cylinder. Eventually, 2.9-liter, 3.2-liter and 4.0-liter versions of this engine would be developed, with the different capacities dictated by changing the stroke from 74.8 to 102 mm, but keeping the bore at 91 mm.

The first cars to use the AJ6 were the 1984 XJ-S line of cars (coupe and cabriolet). The cabriolet was the surprise car. Considered doomed by safety regulations, convertibles were making a small comeback in the automotive marketplace. Jaguar's XJ-SC was a Targa top model with a folding rear window and, as such, wasn't a "real" convertible. But it was Jaguar's first open-topped car in eight years. A later V-12-powered model followed.

In 1986, a true XJ-S Convertible would be announced with a price tag of $50,000. This was not a "factory" car, but was, in fact, an after-market "chopped top" version built by Hess & Eisenhardt in Cincinnati. Customers would buy an XJ-S coupe and have it delivered to H&E, where it would be modified and delivered back to the buyer in 45-60 days. The total price included a three-year, 36,000-mile warranty.

Hess & Eisenhart was one of America's premier coach builders who had built Cadillac limousines since 1936 and had created both Cadillac and Buick convertibles for those manufacturers. Prior to World War II, H&E had built cars designed by Darrin for movie stars.

Two years later, Jaguar introduced its own XJ-S V-12 convertible, with a draft-proof automatic top and stiffened body to eliminate flexing. The XJ-S convertible also had a glass rear window, which incorporated defroster wiring.

This one was built with design assistance from Karmann in Germany, who had designed and built such cars for Volkswagen, Audi and Ford of Germany. Karmann would design and tool the metal expansion frames and folding mechanism. Jaguar would make and fit the fully lined convertible top.

Jaguar had been developing a new sedan for several years. It was not a great secret that the car, code-named XJ40, would be a great new Jaguar sedan. What was a secret, though, was its final name, XJ6. While confusing to those who followed the industry closely, XJ6 was a logical name

to continue for the sedan. Powered by the AJ6 engine, the new XJ6 debuted in September 1986. At the launch, it was announced that the only thing in common between the new XJ6 and its predecessor was the horn button. Comparisons between the BMW 7-series and the Mercedes-Benz S-Class were natural, with the general opinion that the Jaguar and BMW outclassed the S-Class, primarily on the basis of their sportiness

In September 1989, a 4.0-liter version of the AJ6 engine was installed in the XJ6. While horsepower increased from 221 to 235, the real reason for the larger engine was an increase in torque, which went up dramatically from 249 pound feet for the 3.6-liter engine to 285 pound feet for the 4.0. The engine was mated to a new ZF four-speed automatic gearbox with "Sport" and "Normal" modes. Inside, the XJ6 had an instrument panel that returned to round analog gauges in a walnut-trimmed dash.

Jaguar and TWR formed a joint venture, JaguarSport, which developed the XJR-S, introduced in 1989. This car was based on the production XJ-S V-12 coupe, but the 6.0-liter engine now developed 318 horsepower and was mated to a GM three-speed automatic transmission. With a top speed of 160 miles per hour, the XJR-S had a stiffer suspension with better front and rear springs and gas-filled shock absorbers. In addition, the wheels and tires were widened, with the rear tires being wider than the fronts.

Inside, there was Doeskin leather with contrasting piping on the seats, a JaguarSport steering wheel. One hundred Le Mans Celebration cars were specially built and numbered, with Number 2 going to Jan Lammers. His Le Mans-winning Jaguar carried number 2.

A later product of this joint venture would be the 1994 XJR sedan, with a supercharged 6-cylinder engine.

Perhaps the most exciting Jaguar of the decade was the XJ220 concept car. Likely based loosely on the XJ13 concept car, the XJ220 was powered by a 500 horsepower version of the 6.2-liter V-12 engine. Top speed was estimated at over 200 miles per hour, with a 0-60 time of 3.5 seconds. It was unveiled on October 10, 1988, at the Birmingham International Motor Show and caused a sensation.

The frame was built of bonded aluminum with a steel roll cage. The fact that it was 4-wheel drive resulted from a close association with FF Developments, which was a Coventry-based engineering firm owned by 1953 Le Mans winner Tony Rolt. Double wishbones were used for the 4-wheel independent suspension with the rear coil springs in a nearly horizontal position.

But it was also a Jaguar, so it had Connolly leather upholstery and trim on the dash and doors, air conditioning, power windows, adjustable steering column, remote-control locking, heated seats and a CD player. The styling was intended to evoke memories of the XJ13 and E-type.

JaguarSport announced a production run of 220 to 350 cars, depending on demand. The price of the cars was £290,000—about $500,000—and a deposit of £50,000 was required with the order. Firm orders were received from enthusiasts such as Mick Jagger and Elton John, among others.

The production version differed from the concept car in that the engine would be a twin turbocharged version of the V-6 engine used in the XJR-10 and XJR-11 race cars, but detuned to 500 horsepower from 750 horsepower. The production car would also have rear-wheel drive instead of 4-wheel drive. Top speed was still in the 200 miles per hour range, with a 0-60 time of 4.0 seconds.

Jaguar cars also suffered from quality and assembly problems at the end of the decade, just as Customer Satisfaction was becoming a watchword in the industry. With a work force accustomed to doing its job in a more traditional manner in older factories, attention to detail had slipped. Ford's influence would bring tougher quality control guidelines to the factory floor and would bring Jaguar's quality levels, as well as Customer Satisfaction Index values, back to more acceptable levels.

In the United States, sales slipped to 3,023 in 1980, the lowest level they would ever reach. Then vice-president of sales Mike Dale told his staff that they would be wise to explore the job market, because the future of the company was truly questionable. That Dale's predictions were off is attributable to the Series III XJ sedans. Sales were back up to 18,044 by 1984 in a remarkable recovery.

Chapter Seven | The 1990s

Jaguar showed in the 1990s that it was a company that could rebound and still innovate. Customer Satisfaction Index (CSI) ratings rose from a low of 25th overall in 1992 to 9th overall in 1996, an increase attributable to better production methods and a better corporate attitude toward its customers.

Jaguar was also honored when an E-type roadster was made part of the permanent display at the Museum of Modern Art in New York in 1996, recognizing the car's contribution to the world of automobile styling. Only the third automobile to enter the museum's collection, the Malcolm Sayer-designed car was the showpiece

of a four-month exhibit, "Refining the Sports Car: Jaguar's E-type." Terence Riley, chief curator, Department of Architecture and Design, said," Since 1972, when the Museum acquired its first car, a Cisitalia 202 GT, we have been committed to expanding this facet of the design collection. We developed a wish list of ten to twelve cars, with the E-type at the top. Because of the E-type's beauty and sculptural quality, its functionality, and its seminal impact on overall car design, it perfectly suits the criteria of a landmark design object."

In March 1990, Sir John Egan announced that he would be leaving Jaguar in June of that year after ten years as managing director. His contributions to the company were recognized with his Knighthood, conferred in 1986. Egan also presided over the difficult transition from independent company to Ford subsidiary. After his retirement, Bill Hayden was appointed chairman and chief executive at Jaguar by Ford.

1996 XJR
Originally introduced in 1995, the XJR carried a Roots supercharged version of the 4.0-liter V-6 that delivered 322 horsepower and 378 pounds-feet torque. The XJR was developed as a joint venture between Jaguar and Tom Walkinshaw's JaguarSport. It represented Jaguar's first supercharged car. Besides superior performance, the XJR also offered increased levels of luxury over the XJ6, with maple wood trim and a wood-and-leather steering wheel.

1990 JAGUAR XJ6
For the 1990 XJ6 sedan, Jaguar introduced a 4.0-liter version of the AJ6 engine that was based on the original 3.6-liter AJ6. The XJ6 showed only minor changes from the 1989 edition, as the changes were made in the engine compartment. The influence of Ford management had yet to be felt in the design and development of Jaguar cars. Teves anti-lock brakes replaced the Girling/Bosch units formerly used. Quad round headlights were retained on the base model, but rectangular headlights were used for the Vanden Plas, Sovereign and Majestic.

Hayden, a career production man, announced that the pursuit of quality would be unrelenting, and he set out to achieve this on all fronts. The work force was streamlined and contracts re-negotiated to achieve greater worker commitment to building better products. Investments were made in manufacturing facilities, creating improvements in everything from welding to final painting. An increased number of computer-controlled processes ensured accuracy. More robots on the line also contributed to increased accuracy. Qual-

ity standards were set for suppliers as well, and new suppliers were found for parts that didn't measure up. Ford's buying power helped reduce costs.

White coated inspectors, who stood at the end of the line to evaluate cars, were replaced by fault diagnosis on the line itself. Problems were solved at the source so that finished cars could be driven away directly to the transporters. The Uniform Product Assessment System (UPAS) was instituted to ensure that finished Jaguars met the standards of the luxury car buyer, not just production guidelines.

1991 VANDEN PLAS
Only minor changes were reflected in the 1991 XJ6 and Vanden Plas. Both offered leather seats and burl walnut trim, but the Vanden Plas added boxwood inlays in the woodwork and the traditional picnic tables on the rear of the front seats. For 1991, the Vanden Plas was identified by a fluted grille surround and trunk plinth, which were reminiscent of British Daimlers.

In the United States, Jaguar Cars Inc. president Graham Whitehead also retired in 1990 after almost 22 years at the helm. Whitehead had also presided over drastic changes at Jaguar, since he joined the company right after the merger with British Leyland. He was replaced by Mike Dale, who had an equally long tenure and who was responsible for Jaguar's U.S. racing efforts under Bob Tullius. Dale himself was an SCCA champion, driving an Austin-Healey Sprite to that title in 1973.

Dale would direct the company from new North American headquarters in Mahwah, New Jersey. The new facility among the lush foliage of northern New Jersey was a distinct contrast to the Leonia headquarters, which had been inherited from British Leyland Motor Holdings.

On the competition side, Jaguar won Le Mans in 1990, with a TWR XJR-12 driven by John Nielson, Price Cobb and Martin Brundle. It was Jaguar's second win in three years and seventh win overall. The competition season had begun on a strong note as well, with the TWR car winning the Daytona 24 Hours.

In the first half of the decade, Jaguar products were very much the result of Jaguar management; it was only in the latter half of the decade that the influence of Ford began to be felt. Therefore, the company followed a conservative tack with its early vehicles. The first vehicle to be announced was the 4.0-liter version of the XJ6 sedan in September 1990. The engine was based on the 3.6-liter AJ6 engine. Two new models in the sedan range were the Sover-

1991 XJ-S CLASSIC EDITION
Jaguar's 1991 Classic Edition XJ-S Coupe and Convertible both used a 5.3-liter V-12 engine for power, coupled with a 3-speed automatic transmission. The engine was rated at 263 horsepower at 5,350rpm. The XJ-S rode on a 102.0-inch wheelbase and was 191.7 inches long. It weighed 4,050 pounds, but the big V-12 could move it along at a brisk pace. In 1992, Jaguar warranties would increase from three years/36,000 miles to four years/50,000 miles, showing significant confidence in the improved quality of the line.

eign and Vanden Plas Majestic, giving Jaguar four sedan models, all based on the XJ6. The Vanden Plas was an upgrade from the XJ6, with limited-slip differential, self-leveling suspension, headlight washers with heated nozzles, footwell rugs, heated front seats, folding burl walnut picnic tables on the front seat backs, leather-covered seat backs, rear arm rest storage, fog lights and rear reading lamps. The Sovereign added a power sunroof, burl walnut inlays and rear head restraints. The Majestic, which only came in Regency Red, added a magnolia leather interior, diamond-polished alloy wheels and an alarm system.

Base engine for the 1991 XJ-S Coupe and Convertible was the 5.3-liter V-12. A production version of the XJ220 was announced early in 1991, with a turbocharged 3.5-liter V-6. It was priced at £290,000. Jaguar took £50,000 non-refundable deposits on the car and had a full order book. But when the bottom fell out of the collector car market and investors realized that the value of the XJ220 would not appreciate as much as they

had hoped, they tried to reclaim their deposits. Lengthy lawsuits resulted, with Jaguar eventually ending up retaining the deposits.

The last Series III XJ12 sedan left the line at the end of 1992 and went straight to Jaguar's museum. This sedan/engine combination had helped maintain Jaguar's sense of individuality for 20 years, through periods of turmoil. While the V-12 engine may not have been the most practical in an era of fuel crisis and government-mandated fuel economies, it gave Jaguar a definite "halo effect" car whose value far outweighed its negatives.

In 1993, a new sedan range was offered, with approximately one-third new body panels. The changes were made to alter the rigidity for air bag installation. This year, Jaguar identified the Vanden Plas sedan with fluting around the grille and trunk plinth previously used on the short-lived Majestic. This fluting resembled that used on Daimlers. Late in the year, the XJ12 returned with a 6.0-liter V-12 engine.

By 1994, models in the United States were the XJS convertible and coupe with 4.0-liter 6-cylinder and 6.0-liter V-12 engines, the XJ6 and Vanden Plas sedans with 4.0-liter 6-cylinder engines, and the XJ12 sedan with the 6.0-liter V-12. Passenger-side air bags were installed on all models. Prices ranged from $51,750 for the XJ6 to $79,950 for the XJS 6.0L convertible.

By 1995, the first fruits of the Ford investment were realized with a restyled sedan line, a more powerful 6-cylinder engine, and the introduction of Jaguar's first supercharged car, the XJR sports sedan based on the XJ6. The XJR was powered by the 4.0-liter inline six of the XJ6, but with a Roots-type supercharger and a lowered compression ratio. Still, the XJR posted impressive numbers; 322 horsepower at 5,000 rpm and 378 pounds feet torque at 3,050 rpm. XJR carried a price tag

Jaguar's 1994 line was one of the most comprehensive in the company's history. All cars added passenger-side airbags to the driver's side airbags that had been installed since 1993. The sedans were refined with cellular phone pre-wiring, a remote trunk release, and Pirelli P4000E tires on diamond-turned 7x16 aluminum wheels. The XJS line comprised four models, with 4.0-liter 6-cylinder and 6.0-liter V-12 engines in coupes and convertibles.

1996 XJ12

1996 was the last year for the XJ12 sedan. The V-12-engined variation of the X300 was powered by a 6.0-liter engine that was a derivation of the previous 5.3-liter version. With a longer stroke, power was increased as was mid-range torque. The bodyshell had been modified in 1992 to accommodate the V-12 engine, with about 60 of the 140 new or modified panels associated with the V-12 installation. While many of the panels were required for the V-12 engine installation, several were also necessitated by the installation of a driver's-side airbag, including the required chassis stiffening.

of $65,000, just $6,600 more than the base XJ6.

The sedan line was based on the Series III or X300 as it was known internally. The base engine for the sedans was the AJ16, a 4.0-liter inline six based on the AJ6. It developed 245 horsepower, a 10 percent increase over 1994. Exterior styling of the new sedans was smoother and more aerodynamic. As in previous years, grille design differentiated the models.

For 1996, long wheelbase versions of the X300 sedans were introduced. The X300 LWB sedans

rode on a 117.9-inch wheelbase, compared to the standard 113.0-inch wheelbase. In 1996, this chassis was used only for the Vanden Plas and XJ12, but in 1997, with the discontinuance of the V-12-engined car, it became available on XJ6L and Vanden Plas. A short wheelbase XJ6 remained in the line and the XJR kept the short wheelbase as well.

Nicholas Scheele joined Jaguar from Ford of Mexico in 1992 as Chairman and CEO, with the same commitment to quality improvement

1996 XJS
In its last full year of production, the 1996 XJS was offered only as a convertible and only with the 6.0-liter V-12 engine. Coincident with the discontinuance of the XJS, the V-12 engine was also discontinued. The engine of choice for Jaguar's new sports car would be a 4.0-liter V-8, the first V-8 in Jaguar's history. Still the XJs served a useful purpose in Jaguar's history. While not a pure sports car, it provided a continuation of Jaguar sports cars between the E-type and 1997 XK8.

as Hayden. Since taking office, he has pressed for further improvements, including the 21-day installation of a completely new "overhead" sedan assembly track at Browns Lane.

Ford has been relatively true to its initial promise to allow Jaguar to be Jaguar. When the purchase was announced, automotive analyst Maryann Keller said the buy-out was cheap for Ford, because it would have cost them more to develop their own line of luxury cars.

In December 1989, Jack Telnack, Ford vice president of design, told the International Motor Press Association that Ford's plans were to keep Jaguar's uniqueness. Although he also said, "There are so many things that can be done with the XJ6. The proportions are great and the car has a very distinctive silhouette. I would have killed to have that kind of tread and the cowl in that location and the low hood. And now it's right in our laps. We could . . . really clean it up and simplify it."

Chapter Eight | XK8

On the product side, Jaguar returned to the world of exciting sports cars in March and April 1996 with the introduction of the XK8 coupe and convertible, introduced at the Geneva and New York auto shows, respectively. They collected universal praise from all who saw and drove the cars. Nick Scheele said, "The XK8 reaffirms Jaguar's heritage of outstandingly beautiful sports cars. The dynamic style of the XK8 convertible and coupe can only begin to communicate the driving experience in store."

Powered by Jaguar's first V-8 engine, known as AJ-V8, the XK8's introduction meant the departure of its predecessor, the XJS. First intro-

duced in 1975, the XJS was Jaguar's best-selling sports car, with sales of approximately 112,000 units, and was in production longer than any other Jaguar, 21 years.

The AJ-V8 4.0-liter engine is a product of Jaguar's Whitley Engineering Centre in Coventry. It is only the fourth all-new engine designed by Jaguar. It is a four cam, 32-valve, 90-degree V-8 of 3,996 cc capacity that delivers 290 bhp at 6,100 rpm and 284 pounds feet torque at 4,250 rpm. Eighty percent of peak torque is available between 1,400 and 6,400 rpm. At its introduction, the engine represented best-in-class performance in a variety of measures, including specific power output, power density (engine weight versus power), powertrain rigidity and friction levels. Development of the AJ-V8 engine began in the mid-1980s with internal engineering studies that arose out of Jaguar's new-found independence from British Leyland. The first running prototype was produced in November 1991. The engine was benchmarked

The Jaguar XK8 has a wide oval grille that is reminiscent of the E-type. In addition, the modern halogen headlights offer greater candlepower than the sealed-beam headlights of the E-type, while returning to the classic fared in look of the past. The "power bulge" in the hood adds structural stiffness to the panel as well as a muscular look to the first new Jaguar sports car in 30 years.

JAGUAR XK8 COUPE

The 1997 Jaguar XK8 Coupe was introduced at the 1996 New York International Automobile Show to rave reviews. It is a classic aerodynamic design that harkens back to the original E-type of the 1960s with a wide oval grille, fared-in headlights and stunning lines. The XK8 is also powered by Jaguar's first V-8 engine, dubbed AJ-V8. It is only the fourth all-new engine designed by Jaguar. The car and engine were both designed in England. Design of the cars began in the early 1990s, but engine development began in the mid-1980s.

The smooth rear lines of the Jaguar XK8 Coupe hide a respectable 11.1 cubic foot trunk. In addition, there is carrying space behind the front seats. The two rear seats offer head and shoulder room that is only slightly less than that afforded to front seat passengers. The safety-mandated high-mounted stop light is mounted on the rear parcel shelf at the bottom of the windshield.

against the Lexus V-8 for refinement and the BMW V-8 for power delivery.

The square design of the AJ-V8 (86 mm bore x 86 mm stroke) was selected after considerable research with single-cylinder prototypes for its balance of power output with low emissions and high thermal efficiency.

While the 90-degree Vee angle is conventional and the all-aluminum construction is widespread, the die-cast block improves upon standard practice by employing a structural bedplate to establish a rigid, durable foundation for the engine. The bedplate is an intricate aluminum casting that forms the portion of the block below the crankshaft centerline, incorporating the five main bearing caps into a single ladder-type structure. Iron liners are cast in place at each bearing position to ensure that bearing clearance remains constant at all temperatures. Tying the bearing caps (which support the crankshaft) together with the bedplate results in a far stronger engine assembly that not only benefits long-term durability, but also helps to eliminate vibration at the source, improving refinement. It is a feature that is also employed in Cadillac's Northstar V-8 and the Oldsmobile Aurora V-8 that is derived from it and which, in highly modified form, will be one of two powerplants for Indy Racing League cars in 1997.

The working surface of the cylinder bores is formed by an electroplating process called Nikasil (for nickel/silicon carbide), which is applied directly to the aluminum parent material of the engine block. There are no separate iron cylinder liners. A precision casting of spheroidal graphite iron, the crankshaft has minimal bending and twisting under power.

With double overhead camshafts and four valves per cylinder, the AJ-V8 engine cylinder head continues a Jaguar tradition for advanced engine design. The head casting is produced through a proprietary technique developed by Cosworth. The engine's operating efficiency is aided by a narrow included valve angle of just 28 degrees between the intake and exhaust valves, which also contributes to the compact dimensions of the pent-roof combustion chamber.

Jaguar has designed variable cam phasing into the AJ-V8, which offers the midrange benefits of advanced cam timing and the high-speed advantage of retarded valve closing. The timing shift involves only the valve opening and closing points; it doesn't change the duration of the open period or the lift height to which the valve is opened.

Engine management electronics are supplied by Denso, formerly known as Nippondenso, and a company with considerable experience in the luxury market. Nippondenso supplied the management electronics for the 6.0-liter V-12.

Despite a considerable amount of available power, the XK8 does not have a gas guzzler penalty, as the V12 XJS it replaced did.

The all-aluminum AJ-V8 engine is coupled to Jaguar's first five-speed automatic transmission, manufactured by ZF. A unique feature is that the transmission fluid is installed at the factory and never needs to be checked by the owner.

There are two driver-selectable shift modes, Normal and Sport. Switching into Sport makes available a performance-oriented shift program, timing the gear changes for peak response. The transmission also carries a self-regulating "adaptive" feature, which enables it to compensate automatically for the effects of aging and to adjust shift quality based on slippage detected in actual use.

Jaguar's unique "J-gate" selector system is incorporated as well. The driver can operate the transmission in full automatic, or can manually shift between second, third and fourth gears, using the left side of the J-gate.

Front suspension of the XK8 incorporates a short- and long-arm double wishbone system. This style of suspension offers more vertical wheel travel and a greater potential for maximizing tire tread contact with the road. The front suspension is mounted to an aluminum cross-beam casting, which also supports the engine mounts. The use of a cross beam helps prevent noise and vibration generated at the road surface from being transmitted into the engine compartment.

Rear suspension is similar to that used in the XJR sedan. Like the front suspension, it uses a control arm design with coil springs and shock absorber mounted in a single unit. The spring is seated directly on the cast iron transverse lower wishbone, not the shock, which reduces friction to improve ride comfort and noise isolation.

Four-wheel disc brakes are used with a Teves Mk 20 anti-lock braking system. This Teves unit uses an Electronic Control Unit and four wheel-speed sensors. Brakes are 305 mm diameter at all four wheels and are also ventilated at all four wheels to improve resistance to fade and improve wet-weather performance.

The XK8 was designed at the Whitley Engineering Centre under Jaguar Styling Director Geoff Lawson. "One of the key factors in our choice of the coupe design was its ability to translate into a convertible," Lawson said. The fully lined and insulated convertible top retracts to a position slightly above the rear sheetmetal, and can be covered by an easily attached soft cover. Lawson added that, "A design that provides some soft material sitting proud of the sheetmetal is a cue of classic British coachwork. To stow the top under a hard panel would have required raising the rear sheetmetal, a measure not acceptable to us."

"With one-button operation and automatic latching, the XK8's top operation is among the

JAGUAR XK8 ROADSTER
In 1996, Jaguar introduced its first all-new sports car in 30 years, the XK8. The Roadster version exhibits clean aerodynamic lines combined with touches reminiscent of the E-type—wide oval grille, long nose and short tail, and striking performance. What the XK8 offers that the E-type didn't is greater attention to quality and the backing of the Ford Motor Company in the development of the car.

Like the classic British sports cars of the past, the XK8 Roadster's top does not retract completely into the rear deck when it is lowered. Rather, it is covered by a tonneau and is raised slightly above the body, lending a classic touch to this thoroughly modern sports car. Modern safety legislation also requires a high-mounted stop lamp, which is molded nicely into the rear deck lid just under the top. And unlike the classic sports cars of the past, the XK8 does not offer wire wheels as an option. The standard wheels are cast aluminum five-spoke units.

world's best," said chief program engineer Bob Dover. One of the salient features of the XK8 convertible is its fully lined top. Mohair lining and insulation give the XK8 the look and feel of a coupe with the top raised. On the highway at speeds up to 100 miles per hour, there is no wind noise. In fact, the XK8 convertible is in the same class as the famed Lexus LS400 as a quiet-running highway car.

Concept sketches for the XK8 began in 1991. Clay model construction began in January 1992. The final design theme was selected in October 1992.

Wood trim highlights the dash, as in Jaguars of old, and white-on-black analog instruments transmit information to the driver.

Jaguar is marketing the XK8 against the Mercedes-Benz SL500 and BMW 840Ci, and holds a price advantage of approximately $20,000 and $5,000 over those cars, respectively, based on 1997 pricing. The XK8 is still about $12,000 cheaper than the XJS it replaced, when you add in the XJS's $3,700 gas guzzler tax. Advertising debuted on October 3, 1996, with the theme, "A new breed of Jaguar."

As Jaguar cars have been modernized in construction and equipment, they have never lost their traditional looks and performance. Always built with the finest components and unsurpassed luxury, Jaguar products remain the equal of anything on the road in terms of speed, handling and safety. Through Ford's investments in manufacturing facilities and processes, the cars have reached a quality level which firmly ensures that Jaguar's reputation for value will carry on into the next century.

Bibliography

The literature about Jaguar is continually expanding. The books listed below were, in most cases, primary reference sources. Some are included because they are important general reference works for anyone interested in a more in-depth history of the company. Check your Motorbooks International catalog for any recent entries.

Essential Jaguar XK: XK120/140/150. Lawrence, Mike. Bay View Books, 1995.

Jaguar E-Type. Stone, Matthew L. Motorbooks International, 1995.

Jaguar E-Type: The definitive history. Porter, Philip. Automobile Quarterly, 1989.

Jaguar in America. Dugdale, John. Britbooks, 1993.

Jaguar Product Guide. CDI, 1995, 1996, 1997.

Jaguar, Fifth Edition. Lord Montagu of Beaulieu. Quiller Press, 1986.

Jaguar: Catalogue Raisonné 1922–1992. Automobilia, 1991.

Jaguar: History of a classic marque. Porter, Philip. Orion Books, 1988.

Jaguar: The history of a great British car. Whyte, Andrew. Patrick Stephens, Ltd., 1980.

FERRARI

Dennis Adler

Acknowledgments

Ferraris are a passion. They are more, much more than an automobile. For half a century the cars with the yellow and black Cavallino Rampante emblem have represented the ultimate expression of speed and automotive sensuality. Over the years they have been compared with the curvaceousness of a woman's body, the muscular stature of an athlete, and the grace and speed of a thoroughbred. Ferraris have been the benchmark by which all other sports cars have been judged for nearly 50 years.

Within these pages we celebrate the Ferrari legend, that of the man and his machines and all that they have meant to sports car enthusiasts since the early postwar years, when Enzo Ferrari lent his name to the first 125 Sport in 1947.

Names, it seems, have always been a part of the Ferrari legend. The names of engineers such as Gioacchino Colombo and Aurelio Lampredi, designers Carlo Felice Bianchi Anderloni, Giovanni "Pinin" Farina, Sergio Scaglietti, and Mario and Gian Paolo Boano have become as much a part of Ferrari lore as the cars themselves. And lest we forget the greatest Ferraristi of all, the late Luigi Chinetti, without whose efforts there would likely be little, if anything, to write about today.

It is perhaps Ferrari owners who deserve the most credit for having sustained the marque these many years through their continued support of Ferrari and dedication to the restoration and preservation of the early cars. As an author, photographer, and Ferrari enthusiast, I owe a great deal of thanks to collectors such as Robert M. Lee, Skeets Dunn, Ron Pinto, Andy Cohen, William Noon and the staff at Symbolic Motor Car Company, Jerry J. Moore, Bruce Meyer, Tom Reddington, and the late Henry Haga all of whom through their devoted patronage to Ferrari were instrumental in the creation of this book.

If it were possible to write a second dedication, this book would be for my late friend and mentor Dean Batchelor, perhaps one of the greatest Ferrari enthusiasts and historians ever. It was Dean who instilled in me the understanding and respect for the eccentricities of Ferrari, both the man and the cars, and who introduced me many years ago to Sergio Pininfarina, the architect of Ferrari's greatest road cars.

In planning this book, it was decided to pursue the rarest Ferrari road cars, rather than the better-known models, and in so doing we were able to locate and photograph many original prototypes and first production cars, some seen here for the first time in color.

Ferraris are perhaps the most written about but most difficult to understand sports cars in automotive history. It is with great respect that I mention those authors who have wheeled down the path of confusion that leads from Modena's door, most notably the work of Antoine Prunet, who has made understanding Ferrari history a crusade; the late Hans Tanner, who with Doug Nye created the most comprehensive history of the marque ever written; and, of course, Dean Batchelor, whose excellent Ferrari books have become a standard reference the world over.

Additional research for this book came from the remarkable two-volume set, *Ferrari Catalog Raisonne*, published in Italy by Automobilia, and *Ferrari—Design of a Legend, The Official History and Catalog*, by Gianni Rogliatti, Sergio Pininfarina, and Valerio Moretti, published by Abbeville Press.

Others who have contributed to the content of this book include authors T. C. Browne, Denise McCluggage, and Henry Rasmussen. A special note of thanks is also due to Robert M. Lee, Scott Bergan, Skeets Dunn, Luigi Chinetti, Jr., Sergio Pininfarina, and Scott Grundfor for their contributions.

My thanks to one and all for taking part.

Dennis A. Adler, Pennsylvania

Foreword

Ferrari road cars. My first reaction is simply extraordinary. Fifty years of dreams, dedication, and passion. In the following pages you will be presented a tribute and review of a half century of Ferrari the man, the company, and the automobile. It is a story of people—people with a common bond to produce the best racing and performance cars possible.

Shortly after World War II, Enzo Ferrari had decided to build machine tools, much as he had during the war years. Dad [Luigi Chinetti, Sr.] quite naturally opposed this proposition, and in short order he had himself, my mother, and me in Modena on a very cold day in December 1946.

I particularly remember the cold in the buildings at our destination—the necessary frugality of the postwar years. Despite the cold, the decision was made to build road and race cars, provided Dad could supply the clients. He certainly did that, and soon had sold some 12 automobiles to old acquaintances. Some were for the road, and some were for the track. In the latter, he shared the driving tasks with his friends and clients.

Dad won the first endurance race for Ferrari, the 12 hours of Paris. This established Ferrari as an absolutely first-rate competition car. Ferrari's reputation was further solidified by Dad's victories at Le Mans, Spa, and Montlhéry, all events run in 1949. Racing success translated into road car sales.

Not only were the mechanicals race bred, but the stunning designs were the *avante garde* of the Paris, Geneva, and Turin motor shows. Indeed, Italian designers were firmly at the forefront when it came to high-performance automobiles. In short, the Ferrari had confirmed all of the initial aspirations of that small group of visionaries following their passions.

Passion is what makes Ferrari what it is. Ferrari was passionate; my father was passionate. And Modena was passionate, and remains so to this day. The thrill of seeing those early racing cars being tested on the roads around Modena certainly shaped and influenced my life as well.

Outings with Dad when he was trying out a new car were some of the greatest moments of my young life. I went out with many test drivers, Sanesi and Guidotto of Alfa Romeo, Bertocchi of Maserati, and later Michael Parkes of Ferrari. Each had a particular feeling for the car and brought to the end result their particular *imprimatur*.

I deeply regret not being able to bring those years back. Imagine creating those wonderful machines from a clean sheet of paper, choosing engineers like Colombo and Lampredi to design the engines and chassis, and then bringing in the coachbuilders of one's choice to execute one's sculpture.

I remember one June day in 1963 when Dad went to Marenello, along with Mr. Figoni and myself. Figoni was the designer of the beautiful prewar Delahayes and Talbot-Lagos. We were to pick up a 250 Competition short wheelbase coupe and take it to Le Mans over the road. Three in a short-wheelbase berlinetta is difficult at best, and I being the youngest, got the gearbox. Dad firmly believed that testing a car on the road and breaking it in properly were important stages in race car preparation.

Although somewhat biased, I can say that he was probably one of the finest of the *metteurs aux points* in the world. He could bring a car to the highest level of preparation prior to driving it in competition. During all of those 1,000 km, he never missed a shift and was absolutely smooth to a degree that I rarely saw, even in other test drivers—and at 62 years of age!

With the pressure of having to find the necessary funding to go racing, both Dad and Mr. Ferrari had to sell cars on a regular basis. It was with great reluctance that Ferrari acquiesced to building convertibles for the American market. Certainly there had been models called "America," and even "Superamerica," but none was like the California Spyder. It was hard for the factory to understand a convertible as a serious fast car. To them high speed, really high speed, was the domain of the closed car. The California was a wonderful success, and it was followed by the 275 NART Spyder.

For many, the 1960s and early 1970s were the absolute high watermark of the sport and GT automobile. I would certainly subscribe to that. I can still hear those wonderful 3.0-liter sport and GT cars at Sebring, Rheims, Daytona, and, of course, Le Mans—battles with Ford, Porsche, Matra, Alfa and the battles between the Rodriguez brothers, Phil Hill, Gurney, Gendebien, and all the other names.

I look back on the 50 years with great love and sentiment. Ferrari is a story of people and certainly the people of Modena. When I built some of the special NART cars there some six or eight years ago, and I struggled through the Modena winter, I could feel some small kinship with all the people greater than me in whose footsteps I plodded, struggling to bring a new idea to the road.

When people in town would say *"Buon lavoro!"* meaning "Good work!" that said it all: Ferrari and Modena.

Thank you both—Ferrari and Modena—and even greater thanks to my parents for giving me the opportunity to bear witness to these wonderful years.

Congratulations to Dennis Adler for capturing this colorful and productive time and place, and spirit, in this engrossing and beautifully produced book.

Buon Lavoro Ferrari!

Luigi Chinetti, Jr.

Chapter One

The Early Years
Race Cars and Road Cars

It would be difficult to travel anywhere in the world today where the name Ferrari is unknown. In the late 1940s and early 1950s, however, it meant little to anyone not keeping abreast of current events on the European motorsports scene. In Italy, Ferrari's name was already legendary. In 1939, Enzo Ferrari resigned from Alfa Romeo, ending a 20-year career with a company where, at various times, he had served as engineer, factory driver, and finally—through Scuderia Ferrari—the man behind Alfa Romeo's proud racing team.

For most men his age, resignation after so many years with one company would have been prelude to

The car pictured, chassis number 0160 ED, was driven for Scuderia Ferrari in the 1952 Tour of Sicily by Piero Taruffi. The second Vignale Sports Racing Spyder built, 0160 ED bore the traditional styling used on most of the 2.7-liter cars, including the distinctive ovoid portholes cut into the front fenders. One of the most significant styling cues of the 225 S, the portholes were not part of the original design. They were added by Vignale following the Tour of Sicily to improve heat extraction from the engine compartment. At the same time, Vignale removed the car's running lights, and the round openings that had flanked the oval grille were converted to air intakes, creating a new, more aggressive front visage.

retirement, but for the 47-year-old Enzo Anselmo Ferrari it was a reaffirmation of belief in his destiny. Rather than retiring on the laurels of his brilliant career with Alfa Romeo, Ferrari embarked upon a new adventure as an independent industrialist establishing a factory in Maranello. Ferrari later described his decision as proof that during his 20 years with Alfa Romeo, he had "not lived off reflected light, so to speak." Wrote Ferrari, "I wanted to show that the level of notoriety I had reached was a legitimate and hard-earned outcome of my own hard work and of my own aptitudes." Indeed, the accomplishments that had made Scuderia Ferrari renowned throughout European racing circles would establish "Ferrari the auto maker" almost from the moment he opened his doors.

Ferrari established Auto Avio Costruzione and set himself to the task of supervising the design of a new race car. His first examples were commissioned in 1939 by renowned race driver Alberto Ascari and the Marchese Lotario Rangoni Machiavelli di Modena. Completed for the 1940 Grand Prix of Brescia (a replacement for the Mille Miglia that year), neither car bore the Ferrari logo or name. Part of Enzo's contract with Alfa Romeo required that he not build or race cars under his own name for four years. Thus his first

"... small, red, and ugly ..." That was the account one Italian newspaper gave of the first Ferrari. The model pictured, a 166 Spyder Corsa, is not too different in apperance from the 1947 model 125 sports car shown at Piacenza on May 11, 1947. If the shoe fits ...

production car was known simply as Model 815, indicating the number of cylinders and the engine capacity.

Ferrari's four-year, non-competition agreement with Alfa Romeo was comfortably fulfilled during World War II. By 1945, he was free to begin building cars, but by then Italy had lost the war and Ferrari had lost hope, resigning himself to manufacturing machine tools, the modest business which had kept his factory open throughout the war.

Had it not been for the intervention of one man, there might not have been a Ferrari legend. Luigi Chinetti, a prewar comrade, had worked with Ferrari at Alfa Romeo. On Christmas Eve 1946, the 45-year-old Italian race driver and automotive entrepreneur went to see Ferrari. He found him sitting alone in his cold dark office pondering his future, one that in the postwar economy held little promise for Ferrari as a manufacturer of machine tools. He

was at a crossroad, torn between an unfulfilling business and the need to return to that which gave him pleasure, the design and production of sports cars. Europe's postwar economy, however, would not support the kind of automotive business Ferrari had started in 1939.

Chinetti had spent the war years in the United States, becoming a citizen in 1946, before returning that December with his wife and son to visit France and Italy. He had an idea, one that compelled him to drive all the way from Paris to Modena on Christmas Eve. There was indeed a market for European sports cars, not in Europe, but in the United States. He told Ferrari of his plan. "Let's make automobiles," he said. "That is the one thing we are good at." Ferrari considered the idea, and spoke of hiring Gioacchino Colombo, another Alfa Romeo colleague, to develop engines. That night, Luigi Chinetti and Enzo Ferrari

Built on the 88.6-inch wheelbase of the 212, the 225 S was essentially the same layout except for the enlarged engine capacity. The Vignale Spyder body, however, gave this model far more prestige both on and off the race track.

laid the groundwork for the postwar revitalization of *Auto Avio Costruzione*, soon to become *Auto Costruzione Ferrari*.

In creating his first postwar sports cars, Ferrari reasoned that if Maseratis had 4-cylinder engines, Talbots had 6, Alfa Romeos 8, why not 12 then for Ferrari? It was a decision that historian Hans Tanner would later refer to as "... daring and farsighted."

May 11, 1947, was the first time a car bearing the Ferrari name appeared in public. Sports cars were prac-

A trio of 36DCF Weber carburetors delivered the air/fuel mix to the V-12 engine in the 225 Sport. With an 8.5:1 compression ratio, output was 210 hp at 7,200 rpm, discharged to the rear wheels via a five-speed gearbox integral with the engine. The capacity of the Colombo short-block was increased to 2,715cc by taking the bore out to 70 mm. While the engine remained basically Colombo, the roller-type cam followers introduced by Lampredi were used. Most engines also had the 12-intake-port heads.

Stabilimenti Farina produced the first Ferrari cabriolet (011 S) pictured here. This is one of the oldest known road cars, built in 1949, and was displayed at the Geneva Salon by Luigi Chinetti. Geneva was Ferrari's first showing outside Italy. Ferrari had little interest in road cars; it was Luigi Chinetti who convinced Il Commendatore (Enzo Ferrari) to consider the advantages of manufacturing both competition and road-going sports cars. The lines of the car were similar to other Stabilimenti Farina (and Pinin Farina) designs of the time, such as the Alfa Romeo 6C 2500, and were repeated again on the Simca Sport.

ticing for racing at Piacenza, and two versions of the Type 125S 1.5-liter sports car were shown, a simple, two-seat Spyder Corsa, later referred to in an Italian newspaper as "small, red, and ugly," and a roadster with full bodywork by Carrozzeria Touring Superleggera. The 125 S was powered by a 60-degree V-12 engine designed, as Ferrari had suggested, by Gioacchino Colombo.

By 1948, the Ferrari factory was producing a small number of 12-cylinder *competizione* models. One of the earliest examples to wear the yellow-and-black Cavallino Rampante emblem was the Type 166 Spyder Corsa, a simple, cycle-fendered vehicle very similar in appearance to the previous year's Type 125 S and 159 S. That any resemblance to a road car could be found surrounding an early Ferrari chassis was tribute to the Milanese firm of Touring Superleggera.

Convinced by Chinetti of the necessity to offer models with more cosmopolitan appeal to serve the

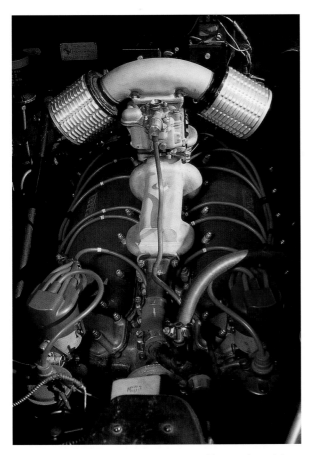

A single carburetor, a unique two-part air filter, and special covers unifying the ignition were characteristics of the first touring Ferraris. This is the original engine from the 166 Inter bodied by Stabilimenti Farina for the 1949 Geneva Salon.

All of the Barchetta bodies—of which Touring built some 46 examples—shared the same sleek, swept-back lines, long hood, short rear deck, and aggressively shaped oval grille, establishing this feature as a Ferrari trait for years to come. The Barchetta's visceral styling would also inspire the the AC Ace and other sports cars of the 1960s. In one bold stroke, Ferrari and Touring had ingeniously closed the distance between race car and road car, without compromising either. Sports cars would never be the same.

Designer Carlo Felice Bianchi Anderloni wrote that the styling of the Barchetta was both a fascinating and courageous undertaking, ". . . fascinating because we were attempting to individualize the Ferrari and not to copy one of the many 'Spider' two-seat sports cars in circulation. Courageous because the results were obtained by overturning the strictest canons of sports car design, which was normally wide at the bottom, narrow at the top and close to the ground." Conversely, the Barchetta had its maximum width just over halfway up the side and visibly high off the ground. It was so different from other sports cars, said Anderloni, that when journalists saw it on the Ferrari stand at the 1948 Turin Salon, they found it necessary to invent the name *Barchetta*, which literally means "small boat." Officially, the cars were cataloged as the 166 Mille Miglia, a name chosen in honor of Ferrari's 1948 victory in the grueling 1,000-mile Italian road race; however, Barchetta was readily used by everyone, even Ferrari.

The Touring design was not only revolutionary in form, utilizing the firm's exclusive "Superleggera" or "super-light" construction method of small, lightweight steel tubes to which the body panels were attached, but in its color scheme as well, sheathed in a unique blend of slightly metallicized red. Most of the 166 MMs were painted this color, which has become a Ferrari tradition. Virtually every Barchetta was a race car, whether *competizione*, powered by the 140-hp Export V-12, or *lusso*, with the 110-hp Inter V-12.

The 166 Mille Miglia was arguably the fastest sports car in the world at the time, and with it, Scuderia Ferrari's cannonade across Europe recorded more than 80 overall or class victories between April 1948 and December 1953.

needs of both road and track, Ferrari again retained Touring to create sports car bodies, this time to complement the unattractive but successful cycle-fendered Spyder Corsas that had become standard Ferrari fare. A year later, the first "sports car" design ever shown on a Ferrari chassis was introduced—the 166 Touring Barchetta. Few cars in automotive history have left such a lasting impression on the motoring world.

Almost 50 years after its debut, it is still considered among Ferrari's most admired models. The styling of the Barchetta was based in part on the BMW 328 Spyder, designed by Carrozzeria Touring in 1940.

The 166 Touring Barchetta was the first "sports car" design ever shown on a Ferrari chassis. The aggressive stance of the body was set atop the patented Superleggera welded tubular steel frame on a wheelbase of 86.6 inches. Track measured 49.8 inches front and 49.2 inches rear. The front suspension was Ferrari's independent A-arm design supported by a single transverse leaf spring. The rear utilized a live axle with semi-elliptic springs and parallel trailing arms on each side. Shock absorbers were the Houdaille hydraulic lever action type. The car pictured was originally raced by Luigi Villoresi and later sold to race driver and Ferrari importer Luigi Chinetti.

It was Chinetti who brought Ferrari its first significant postwar racing victory co-driving a 166 MM Touring Barchetta with Britain's Lord Peter Selsdon in the 1949 Vingt-Quatre Heures du Man. "Iron Man Chinetti" drove 23 of the 24 hours to clinch Ferrari's first and most important international win. Chinetti

Interior of the 166 Barchetta featured beautiful, hand-sewn leather upholstery and trim. Simplicity of design was purely race bred. The cars were considered luxe, or *lusso,* when given the full interior treatment. Note the five-speed shifter which has the gears lettered in Roman numerals.

The Colombo-designed 60-degree V-12 used in the 166 MM Touring Barchetta was as beautifully styled as the body surrounding it. With a displacement of 1,995cc (122ci), output was 140 hp at 6,600 rpm. A 60.0x58.8-mm bore and stroke (2.362x2.315 inches) and compression ratio of 10:1 were fueled by three Weber 32 DCF twin-choke, downdraft carburetors.

went on to win the Spa-Francorchamps 24-hour race for touring cars the following July. In 1950, Alberto Ascari won the Grand Prix du Luxembourg and the Silverstone International Trophy. Dorino Serafini and Luigi Villoresi came in second at Silverstone driving a single-carburetor Barchetta, in all probability the very car pictured in this book, which was sold to Chinetti and later to American driver Bill Spear.

The differences between race car and road car were all matters of interpretation. The Barchetta was stunning but far from practical. It was strictly a fair-weather car. What Ferrari needed for the road was a convertible, and he turned to Stabilimenti Farina to build the first Ferrari cabriolet, chassis 011 S. The first convertible road car to wear the Ferrari badge made its debut at the 1949 Geneva Salon.

With the obvious exception of the roof, the convertible's design was almost identical to the 166 coupe, except for a flatter trunk, made necessary by the cabriolet top. The lines were simple and quite typical of Italian designs of the period. Aside from

The 1951 Ferrari 212 was one of Maranello's first road cars. Many of the 212 bodies were produced by Carrozzeria Vignale and are considered among the most attractive of all early berlinettas. When the opportunity arose to build Ferrari's first noncompetitive model, Vignale and Michelotti penned designs that, while they may not have been altogether original, were executed to a level of quality few others were able to duplicate.

A hybrid combination of 212 Inter and Export, this luxurious Vignale coupe was equipped with the competition gas tank, fuel filler, and exposed spare but with the luxurious trim and upholstery of the noncompetition model. Chassis 175 E, it is believed, though not documented, competed in the 1951 Carrera PanAmericana.

By the early 1950s, Ferrari road cars were growing in number, and most of Italy's leading design houses were producing coachbuilt bodies to fit the new 212 Inter. Ferrari first turned to Carrozzeria Pinin Farina in 1952 to design a stylish sport cabriolet. The design, as would be expected from the avant-garde drafting board of Battista "Pinin" Farina, established a new styling trend with flat-sided body panels. The shape of many later sports car designs can be seen in this first Pinin Farina Ferrari.

the grille and bumpers, this first Ferrari cabriolet resembled the early postwar Alfa Romeo 6C 2500 Sport, designed by coachbuilder Pinin Farina, and the basic body lines of both cars were not too distant from those of the 1947 Cisitalia, also by Pinin Farina. The prototype cabriolet was purchased by Italian film director Roberto Rossellini.

One of the significant turning points in Ferrari road car production came in 1951, with the introduction of the Type 212. The 212 Berlinetta marked the beginning of a new era at Maranello. Where racing had once been Ferrari's sole *raison d'être*, the

design and production of *boulevardiers* had now taken on equal importance. Not everyone enthralled by illusions of the Ferrari's V-12 and exhilarating performance wanted to race, nor suffer the discomfort of a built race car's purpose-built interior and cockpit.

Although Ferrari considered competition his first priority, and had little, if any, interest in road cars, Chinetti convinced him that one could feed upon the other. Ferrari finally agreed with Chinetti's logic. The race cars improved the road cars, and the profits from their sales financed the development of race cars. Indeed, a competition engine could be

The 166 MM chassis were also fitted with a variety of coachbuilt designs by Italy's leading design houses, including a coupe by Allemano, an Inter coupe by Touring, an early berlinetta bodied by Stabilimenti Farina, and sport berlinettas produced by both Vignale and Touring Superleggera. The styling of the Touring Barchetta influenced this stunning berlinetta by Touring, produced in 1950. *Automobile Quarterly*

detuned for the street. And as for bodies, in postwar Italy, there was no shortage of coachmakers available to clothe the V-12's chassis. Bespoke coachwork from Italy's leading designers graced a number of early Ferrari chassis with exquisite two- and four-place creations such as Touring's 166 Inter coupe, the Ghia 212 Inter, and Pinin Farina's stunning Type 342 America of 1953.

Among the most stylish of early Ferrari road cars were those built by Vignale. The luxurious Vignale 212 Inter was intended as a touring car but also managed to do quite well when pressed into

competition. A pair of 212 Inters finished first and second in the 1951 Carrera Panamericana, with Piero Taruffi and Luigi Chinetti in the lead car and Alberto Ascari and Luigi Villoresi close behind. The 212 could also be ordered in a stripped-down Export or *competizione* version. Even when built for racing, the Vignale was a car with striking *savoir-faire*. In all, it is estimated, and only estimated, since the assignment of serial numbers in the early years was less than precise, that around 80 Type 212 Inter (noncompetition models) were built and another 27 Exports (racing).

The 212 Inter's engine displaced 2,562.51cc (156.3ci), fueled by three Weber 36DCF carburetors. Output was rated at 180 hp at 7,000 rpm with 8:1 compression. (Some figures show 170 hp at 6,500 rpm.) Earlier engines had one 36 DCF Weber twin-choke carburetor and developed 130 hp at 6,000 rpm. The 60-degree V-12 was fitted with a light alloy cylinder head and block, special cast-iron pressed-in liners, an increased bore of 68 mm (2.68 inches), and the standardized stroke of 58.8mm (2.315 inches). Power was delivered via a five-speed non-synchromesh with direct drive in fourth gear.

As production of road cars progressed, interior treatments became more luxurious and the use of leather to cover door panels and the transmission tunnel more common. Aside from the instrument panel and the basic outline of the dashboard, interior decor was at the discretion of the individual coachbuilder and client.

The Vignale Inter represents the quintessence of the Italian coachbuilder's art in the 1950s. And it is here that the true romance of Ferrari's early years can be seen. There is so much handwork that one must study even the smallest appointments to appreciate the workmanship; hand-tooled door pulls with small Vignale cloisonnés; chromed window moldings and trimwork; hand-sewn leather and fabrics. In virtually every detail, inside and out, this was the work of artisans practicing skills that have long since been replaced by production-line robotics or have simply become costly anachronisms.

Among the more striking designs on the 212 Inter was the first collaboration between Ferrari and Pinin Farina, a cabriolet on chassis 0117 E delivered June 17, 1952. It was a low-line two-seater distinguished by a grille of generous dimensions, a hood with double air intakes, and a sweeping integrated fenderline that combined a subtle but distinctive return of the tail-light pod into the rear fender.

In the early 1950s, the distinction between road car and race car was still of little consequence, and

several of Ferrari's most alluring *competizione* also made superb berlinetta and spyder versions for the road. Of the latter, the short-lived Type 225 S stands out as one of Maranello's most intriguing dual-purpose models. How then did one distinguish between a Ferrari race car and a Ferrari sports car? If Tazio Nuvolari was driving, it was a race car.

With sports cars continually profiting from the lessons of the race track, the outcome was often an interim model like the 225 S. While the Barchetta would become the most popular Ferrari body style on the Types 166, 195 S, and 212 chassis, the 225 S was by far the most exciting open car of the early 1950s. A listing of serial numbers shows that about 20 were built during the car's single year of production, 1952, and that all but one had coachwork by Vignale—twelve spyders and seven berlinettas. Of those, around half-a-dozen had the Tuboscocca form of chassis/frame with double outer tubes, one above the other joined by a truss-like arrangement, with additional tubing used to create a skeleton outline of the body shape to which hand-formed panels could be mounted.

With its top lowered, the Pinin Farina cabriolet shows off its sleek, sporty styling lines, a fast fender sweep to the rear, accented only by the wheel arches, and a subtle but distinctive return of the taillight pod into the rear fender. The slight curve into the rear fender was the only line breaking up the car's profile.

The 225 Sport followed the design of the 212 Inter, with a Colombo short-block V-12 bored and stroked to 70x58.8 mm and a cubic capacity of 2.7 liters.

Essentially an engine variation, the 225 S shared the 212's chassis, with double wishbone, transleaf spring front, and rigid axle semi-elliptic spring rear suspension, with the same physical dimensions: a wheelbase of 88.7 inches with front and rear tracks of 50.4 inches and 49.25 inches, respectively. The only notable difference was that the 225 S used 5.25x16 tires at the front compared to the 212 Inter's 5.50x16. Rear tires were identical at 6.50x16. It was the car's styling, more than anything else, that set it apart from other Ferraris of the period.

In May 1952, the car originally driven for Ferrari by Piero Taruffi was sold through a dealer in Rome to Roberto Bonami, who campaigned the 225 Sport throughout South America, winning the 1953 Buenos Aires 1,000-km race and the Argentine Sports Car Championship in both 1952 and 1953. Two years later, on January 23, 1955, this same car finished sixth overall in the 1,000 km of Buenos Aires. It has led what most would call a charmed life—never crashed, never abused, still with its original engine, and in good hands from the day it was built.

It's unlikely that Taruffi's car will ever again visit the abusive pavement of a road course, but like all great things past, this composite of steel and alloy has become greater than the sum of its parts. An icon. Something Enzo Ferrari probably hadn't envisioned in 1947, when his cars were merely "small, red and ugly."

Chapter Two

Carrozzeria
Ferrari and the Italian Ateliers

By the mid-1950s, Ferrari was producing a substantial number of road cars, and the separation between these cars and those built for competition was becoming more clearly defined. However, to say that there were production Ferraris was still a bit of a stretch. The design and construction of bodies remained the work of the individual carrozzeria, although Ferrari had by now settled on Pinin Farina and Vignale as his two most-often called-upon coachbuilders.

The rarest and most desirable Ferrari road car ever produced was the 250 GTO. Introduced in 1962, this became the quintessential road/race car of the era. The bodies were produced for Ferrari by Scaglietti, and a total of 39 were built in 1962, 1963, and 1964. Essentially a refined 250 GT SWB Berlinetta, the cars were equipped with a modified 250 GT engine, six twin-throat Weber 38DCN carburetors, a five-speed all-synchromesh gearbox replacing the old four-speed, and a potent 300-horsepower output at 8,400 rpm. Noted Hans Tanner, ". . . the car was for all intents and purposes, a Testa Rossa with a roof." In order to be homologated, Ferrari was supposed to produce 100 examples; however, when pressed by the FIA, Il Commendatore said that the market for the car was already saturated and there were only a few men in the world who could master its ferocity! The FIA still granted Ferrari homologation for the 1963 and 1964 seasons. *Automobile Quarterly*

Vignale catered to a number of prominent postwar Italian auto makers. The carrozzeria was not that old, at least compared to many of its competitors such as Touring and Pinin Farina.

The Vignale brothers had established a small workshop in Turin's Grugliasco district in 1939; but it was not until after the war that Vignale became successful.

Vignale had moved to Turin, taken in a partner, Angelo Balma, and a young designer named Giovanni Michelotti. Within two years, Carrozzeria Vignale had become a recognized car body designer, and through the firm's work for Ferrari in the early 1950s, rose to international fame. From 1950 to 1953, the Vignale works produced bodies for Ferraris that won three Mille Miglia and one Carrera Panamericana.

During the early part of the 1950s, Ferrari road cars varied from the 212 series (which remained in production until October 1953) through the 340 America (1951-1952), 342 America (1952-1953), and the 375 America, introduced in 1953. These were the first road cars to successfully carry the Ferrari name beyond Italy, particularly in the United States, where Luigi Chinetti was establishing Ferrari as the most prestigious line of sports and racing cars in the country.

The Cisitalia, designed in 1947 by Battista Farina became the basis for virtually every sports car design of the late 1940s and early 1950s. The earliest Ferrari road cars resembled this design, as did the first Ferrari cabriolet. The Cisitalia introduced the ovoid grille, fender port holes, and fastback styling that would become familiar on Italian sports cars like the Ferrari 166 and 212.

Chinetti had some pretty tough competition in the early 1950s. Sharing the New York spotlight was automotive importer Max Hoffman, with his plush Frank Lloyd Wright-designed showroom in the heart of New York City and a line of stunning new sports cars from Porsche, BMW, and Mercedes-Benz. Like Chinetti, Hoffman had the pulse of America's sports car elite, and the battle for sales was fought all the way from the showroom floor to the pits of Watkins Glen.

At the same time Ferrari was building the 212 Inter and Export, he decided to add a larger car that would appeal more to the American market and serve as the basis for a new competition car capable of taking on the Cadillac- and Chrysler-engined Allards, which were now showing their tails to the smaller-engined Ferraris. The old adage that there is no substitute for cubic inches was proving itself true once again.

By the mid-1950s Ferrari would introduce the 410 Superamerica as a response to Detroit's high-

Carrozzeria Touring's design for the legendary 166 MM was not only revolutionary in form, utilizing the firm's exclusive "Superleggera" or "super-light" construction method of small, lightweight steel tubes to which the body panels were attached, but in its color scheme as well, sheathed in a unique blend of slightly metallicized red. Most of the 166 MMs were painted this color, which has become a Ferrari tradition. The 166 MM chassis were also fitted with a variety of coachbuilt designs by Italy's leading houses, including a coupe by Allemano, an early berlinetta bodied by Stabilimenti Farina, and sport berlinettas produced by both Vignale and Touring Superleggera. *Automobile Quarterly*

The short-lived 340 America and 342 America were replaced in 1953 by the improved 375 America. The 375 was truly directed at the American market and Luigi Chinetti's New York City clientele. Many of the models, such as this Vignale Cabriolet, were designed for touring, rather than competition. Vignale bodied only two or three chassis in the 375 series. Chassis 0353 AL was fitted with an "American" windshield typical of the period. *Automobile Quarterly*

power V-8s. The road from 212 to Superamerica, however, was paved with interim models, a handful of rare and exceptional cars built in limited numbers from 1952 to 1956.

Among the early high-performance coachbuilt cars was the 340 America, a model that proved moderately successful; although of the 22 constructed, only 8 were road cars. It was followed in the winter of 1952–53 by the more luxurious 342 America. Like its predecessor, the 342 offered left-hand drive. (It was during the production of late 212 models that the first left-hand-drive Ferraris were built. Until then, road cars had shared the same right-hand-drive layout as competition models.)

The 342 series was short-lived, concluding after only six examples—a stopgap between the 340 America and the new 375 America. The 375 had its engine capacity increased to 4.5 liters (275.8 ci) with a bore and stroke of 84x68 mm (3.307x2.68 inches) and three twin-choke Type 42DCZ Webers replacing the 40DCF used on the 342 America.

It had been designed principally for Chinetti's North American clientele, whereas the companion 250 Europa, also introduced in 1953, was intended for the European market. Both models made their debut at the Paris Auto Salon in October and, except for engines, were almost identical. The Europa had a 3-liter V-12. Production of the 375 America ended in

Among the more eclectic designs on the 410 Superamerica was a Ghia show car inspired by the carrozzeria's collaboration with American designer Virgil Exner and Chrysler. Ghia produced an entire series of concept cars for Exner, and stylist Mario Savonuzzi resumed the theme originally created for Exner's Gilda and Chrysler Dart concept cars with the 410 Superamerica. This was the most "Americanized" Ferrari ever produced.

1954 after approximately 13 cars were built, the majority of which were bodied as coupes by Pinin Farina.

For Americans, the construction of coachbuilt cars was a thing of the past, as outdated in the 1950s as a Duesenberg. In Europe, the advent of unitbody construction was also diminishing the demand and capability for producing bespoke coachwork. Ferrari, however, was an exception, still building cars in the manner of a decade before, delivering rolling chassis to local carrozzeria. Early on, Ferrari had relied on Touring and Stabilimenti Farina for designs. The latter, which opened its doors in 1905, was one of the oldest body builders in Turin. From Farina came such talented designers as Mario Boano, Giovanni Michelotti, and of

course, Battista Farina, who established his own carrozzeria in 1930. Beginning in 1950, Pinin Farina took the place of Stabilimenti Farina, which closed its doors. Battista Farina and his son, Sergio, began working closely with Maranello to design coachwork equal to the expectations of Ferrari owners.

The 410 Superamerica was a road car in the fullest sense, as its size and weight, an average of 3,500 lb, would have given it a decided handicap in racing. The handling and ride characteristics of the 410 Superamerica were better suited to vast open highways and cross-country touring than to winding mountain roads and city traffic. Given a good stretch of blacktop, the 4.9-liter V-12 could propel the 410 well into triple digits.

The Superamerica's interior was more finely detailed than any previous Ferrari model. The car used a four-speed synchronized (Porsche-type) transmission but with different gear ratios than the 375 America. The most disconcerting feature of the transmission was that on the majority of cars, first gear was found forward and to the right, and fourth was back and to the left.

The engine design on the 410 Superamerica was similar to the ones employed on the 1951 F1 and on all sports cars until 1954. Displacement, however, was brought to the 5.0-liter limit through the use of new liners. The Lampredi-designed, long-block, 60-degree V-12 displaced 4,962 cc with a 88x68-mm bore and stroke, 8.5:1 compression ratio, and output of 340 hp at 6,000 rpm.

Recalls Sergio Pininfarina, (the coachbuilder had formally changed the spelling of its name in 1958, after the design firm opened new facilities in Grugliasco, outside of Turin). "After the war, in 1947, my father designed the best car he ever did, the Cisitalia. I think it set the pace for the design of sports cars throughout the next decade."

Indeed, it is virtually impossible to look at any European sports car designed in the 1950s and not see some resemblance to the Cisitalia. "As I look at it today it is still so simple, so well proportioned, a masterpiece, difficult to add anything to. . . ." said Pininfarina.

The 1950s were an important period for the Pinin Farina factory as it began to work with Ferrari. "In Italy, I would say we began to work with all the automobile manufacturers, and in Europe, with Peugeot, in England British Leyland, and some Japanese firms. My father was also the first Italian to design an American-built car, the Nash Ambassador," adds Pininfarina with a note of pride. But it was Enzo Ferrari who brought the most prominence to Pinin Farina—not for the volume of work Maranello provided, but rather for the adulation each new design received. Pinin Farina has since designed almost every Ferrari road car produced in the last 45 years!

Explains Sergio Pininfarina, "My inclination for sports cars is understood when you realize that when I was 25 years old, in 1951, my father gave me responsibility of the Ferrari section. Can you imagine a young engineer being responsible for the relation with Mr. Ferrari? He was a difficult man, a great man, a man that, with my father, gave me my point of reference for the love and dedication to automobiles."

The car's elegant profile was accentuated by a wraparound backlight, slightly finned rear fenders, and a distinctive rear fender cleave that swept downward to the rockers, creating a sweep panel effect from the doors forward. The Pinin Farina design for the 410 Superamerica also incorporated side vents located just aft of the front wheel openings. They had been common on competition cars and had been seen on the one-off Farina 250 GT Berlinetta at Paris, but this marked the first application on a Ferrari road car. They would become a trademark of the Superamerica and subsequently appear on nearly all Ferraris.

The production 250 MM carried on the Ferrari practice of independent front suspension with unequal length A-arms and transverse leaf spring. The rear setup was still a live axle, two semi-elliptic springs, and twin parallel trailing arms on each side which took braking and acceleration torque in addition to positioning the axle. The wheelbase, measuring 94.5 inches, was the shortest Ferrari had built since the 212 Export at 88.6 inches and the 166 MM at 86.6 inches. The front and rear track were identical to the 225 Export and 225 MM at 51.5 inches and 52.0 inches, respectively.

The cockpit of the 250 MM was just that, a place for the *pilota*, a traditional right-hand-drive racing configuration with two large combination gauges, bucket-type seats, and a large, wood-rimmed steering wheel. The 250 MM was equipped with a new four-speed all-synchromesh transmission.

Although Pinin Farina had created several significant cars for Ferrari by 1956, the design of the 410 Superamerica was perhaps the most important in cementing the bond between these two great companies. The 410 Superamerica was one of the most dynamic road car designs of the decade. Throughout Ferrari's first half century, few cars have been as influential in the world of automotive design.

The debut of Maranello's latest road car turned more than a few heads. The styling of the Superamerica would become the foundation for the 250 GT PF coupe, the original 250 GT Berlinetta "Tour de France" design, and would influence strongly the 250 GT Cabriolet and Spyder California with its distinctive rear fender kick-up.

Displacement for the 250 MM engine was 2,953cc (180ci) with a 73x58-mm bore and stroke (2.870x2.315 inches) and compression of 9.2:1. The Colombo-designed V-12 had 12 intake ports with the plugs on the outside of the heads. The air/fuel mix was delivered via three Weber 36 IFC/4 twin-choke, downdraft carburetors.

Above and Right
While each 250 MM varied in appearance, 0332 MM was highly distinguished by Vignale's use of faired-in headlights, a front-leaning stance, and foreshortened front fenders. Notable Vignale traits were the front wing, portholes, triangular vents in the rear fenders, and air ducts in the rocker panels.

Preceding the 410 Superamerica was a 375 concept car displayed at the Turin auto show in 1955. The styling of this sensational coupe, in white with contrasting black roof, clearly predicted the bodylines and color scheme of Pinin Farina's forthcoming 410 Superamerica show car. Renowned Ferrari historian Antoine Prunet, wrote that the 410 ". . . represented important progress in the design of the engine, the chassis, and the body."

As a bare chassis and engine displaying Ferrari's latest developments, the 410 Superamerica was shown at the Paris Salon in October 1955 and with

The 250 GT Berlinetta "Tour de France" was introduced for the 1956 racing season. Powered by a Colombo-based 60-degree V-12, developing 260 hp at 7,000 rpm, the Tour de France became Ferrari's customer competition model. All of the cars in this series had odd serial numbers, making them "production" road cars. They received FIA homologation because the mechanical specifications were identical to the Boano/Ellena coupes being built at the same time. Later "Tour de France" models (1958) had a redesigned front end more closely styled to the 250 GT Spyder California. *Automobile Quarterly*

the Pinin Farina body the following February. As a successor to the 375, the 410 used many of the same components along with the very successful Lampredi-designed V-12 engine that had won the 24 Heures du Mans, the Buenos Aires 1,000 km, and the Pan American road race.

The Lampredi V-12, increased to almost 5 liters, was given new cylinder barrels of an extreme 88-mm (3.46-inch) bore, while the 68-mm (2.68-inch) stroke was retained, giving the engine a displacement of 4,961.576cc (302.7ci). Using three twin-choke type 42DCZ Weber downdraft carburetors and a compression ratio of 8.5:1,

the 60-degree V-12 now delivered 340 hp at 6,000 rpm, and later versions, produced in 1958 and 1959 with 9:1 compression, developed a staggering 400 hp at 6,500 rpm. Of course, at this point in history, Ferrari was planning to sell cars in the United States where the horsepower wars raged and cars with such power were almost the *sine quahon*. However, for Ferrari, this was the largest displacement engine to yet power a touring car.

The chassis design of the 410 employed designs already in use on the 250 GT, specifically the front suspension, where the single transverse leaf spring used to

A factory-built steel-bodied car, this 250 GT SWB Berlinetta is reputed to have been a hill-climb racer fitted with the Type 168 competition motor, ribbed gearbox, larger carburetors, higher compression pistons, the big fuel tank, external quick-fill gas cap, and quick-lift jacks. Something of a hybrid, it combines competition and lusso traits. However, this car is definitely set up for competition. Not unusual in the early 1950s, but less common in the 1960s.

support the A-arms on the 375 was replaced by coil springs, as had been done on the Europa GT. Both the front and rear track were also increased from the 375 by 130 mm to 58.4 inches and 58.2 inches, respectively. Chassis length remained at 110 inches until the 1958 and 1959 models, which were reduced to 102.3 inches.

Although no two 410 Superamericas were exactly alike, those bodied by Pinin Farina were similar in appearance and considered the most aggressive yet offered on a Ferrari road car.

In 1956, the 410 Superamerica was without peer, except for the Mercedes-Benz 300SL, and then only in terms of styling. In performance and price, the Ferrari was alone in its class. At the New York Auto Show, a 410 Superamerica of nearly identical design to the Belgian show car was offered by Chinetti at $16,800. The Mercedes-Benz 300SL from Max Hoffman was nearly $10,000 less.

With such a high price it is no wonder only 14 Superamericas were produced. Ghia and Boano also produced coachwork for this model: Ghia one coupe—the radical Chrysler Gilda and Dart-inspired 410 Superamerica, and Boano a convertible and a coupe. Pinin Farina also prepared a luxury custom-built

The interior of the production 250 GT SWB Berlinettas was plush for a competition-based design. This example has unusual dark green leather upholstery, an interesting contrast to the bright yellow exterior.

model, the Superfast I, No. 0483 SA. This was a very special coupe on a shortened 410 SA chassis which had been fitted with the twin-ignition racing engine used in the Scaglietti-bodied 410 Sport spyders. Other features of the Grugliasco designer's genius on this car were faired headlights, the large oval grille, and pillarless windscreen.

Well into the 1950s, the race car and road car were still relatively interchangeable. Early in 1952, Ferrari had decided to continue development of the short-block Colombo-designed V-12, even though the larger long-block Lampredi engine had been successfully converted from a 4.5-liter Grand Prix engine into a sports car powerplant.

Since its introduction, Ferrari had continually improved upon the original Colombo-designed V-12, increasing the displacement from an initial 1.5 liters to

2.7 liters. In the spring of 1952, another manipulation of the bore and stroke resulted in doubling the engine's original swept volume.

The new 250 Sport engine, while maintaining the stroke at 58.8 mm (2.32 inches), had the bore increased from 70 mm to 73 mm (2.875 inches), for a total displacement of 2,953cc (180ci). This new engine was fitted with pistons giving a robust 9.0:1 compression ratio, and when paired with three Weber 36 DCF carburetors was capable of producing 230 hp at 7,500 rpm.

The revised engine was mounted in a Vignale-bodied Berlinetta similar in appearance to the older 225 Sport, and this was the car Giovanni Bracco drove to victory in the 1952 Mille Miglia.

Ferrari historian Hans Tanner described the 1952 Italian road race as one of the greatest battles in the history of motor racing, as Bracco took on the whole of the Mercedes-Benz team. Up against bad weather and the incomparable Karl Kling driving a 300SL, Bracco battled for the lead, gaining and losing it several times until the final leg of the race over the Futa Pass. "Using his knowledge of the treacherous road," wrote Tanner, "Bracco caught up with and passed the Mercedes. When he reached Bologna at the foot of the pass, he was four minutes ahead of Kling, a lead he maintained for the balance of the race through Modena, Reggio, Emilia and Piacenza." This was the only defeat Mercedes-Benz suffered in the 1952 season.

Convinced by the success of the 250 Sport during a full season of racing, Ferrari decided to put this newly developed engine into a series-built chassis. However, time was short, and at the 1952 Paris Motor Show only a bare chassis and engine were displayed. Nevertheless, the 250 Sport's legendary season was enough to generate orders for a production version. The Paris Motor Show chassis was sold in the fall of that same year to Italian movie director Roberto Rossellini and given to Carrozzeria Vignale for completion as a competition spyder.

The production 250 MM was equipped with 12-port heads and three four-choke 36 IFC/4 Webers. Output was increased from the 250 Sport's 220 hp at 7,000 rpm to 240 hp at 7,200 rpm. The 250 MM was produced in both berlinetta and spyder configurations with the majority in berlinetta form bodied by Pinin

Farina. A total of 12 spyders were built by Vignale in two distinct series.

At the time, Ferrari had looked upon the 250 Sport merely as a normal evolution of a well-proven and time-tested design. But rather than the last throes of the old Colombo engine, the 250 Sport marked the beginning of Ferrari's longest-running series: the 250 GT. For nearly a decade, some 3,500 motors of almost identical design would power road car and race car alike.

Within Ferrari lineage, the 250 GT SWB Berlinetta was one of those rare cars afforded legendary status by sports car enthusiasts from the day of its introduction. It was simply the right car at the right moment, introduced on the heels of one great design—the 250 GT Berlinetta "Tour de France"—and preceding an even greater car—the Ferrari 250 GTO. The 250 GT SWB Berlinetta was the bridge between two of Ferrari's most significant road and race cars of the 1950s and 1960s.

The design for the 250 GT Berlinetta "Tour de France" followed the tragic Mercedes-Benz 300SLR accident at Le Mans in 1955, where driver Pierre Levegh and 80 spectators were killed after his failed attempt to avoid hitting a slower car. This horrible accident marked a turning point for sports car racing, which by 1955 had progressed to the point where competition sports cars were closer to Grand Prix cars than road cars. As a result, the Federation Internationale de l'Automobile (FIA) created new racing classes under the title Grand Touring. With help from Pinin Farina, Ferrari was ready to compete in the GT category with a brand new sports car, the 1956 250 GT Berlinetta.

A berlinetta ("little sedan" in Italian) was a lightweight, streamlined body trimmed for racing. Interiors were afforded minimal trim, insulation, and accessories, making them louder and less comfortable, but not unbearable. As each car was essentially built to order, some were more luxuriously appointed than others.

The "Tour de France," a name affectionately given the early 250 GTs following their domination of the 10-day race in 1956, remained in production until 1959, by which time the new SWB Berlinetta was waiting in the wings.

A quick change to colder plugs, racing tires, and the addition of a roll bar, and the 250 GT SWB Berlinetta could stand its ground against purpose-built racers in any sports car event from the Tourist Trophy at Goodwood to the 24 Hours of Le Mans.

Far removed from the competition scene was another Ferrari also called 250 GT, a pure road car produced by Pininfarina. The 250 GT PF coupe became the first standard-production Ferrari sports car. Thus, the Gran Turismo initials have been variously applied to a number of Ferraris. The 250 GT SWB Berlinetta, however, was by no means a production car.

Giotto Bizzarrini, Carlo Chiti, and Mauro Forghieri had completed development of the prototype in 1959, using a shortened 94.5-inch wheelbase. The new car used a solid rear axle, but it was located in such a way that an independent rear suspension would have provided no advantage. The front suspension used wishbones and coil springs with an antiroll bar.

The rigid rear axle used leaf springs and radius arms.

Bizzarini's goal had been to improve the handling of the long-wheelbase 250 GT, and this he accomplished with the SWB Berlinetta. Although the pure road cars (lussos) were more softly sprung, the hard suspension of the competition version gave the 250 SWB terrific cornering power.

Ferrari unveiled the 250 GT SWB Berlinetta at the Paris Auto Show in October 1959. On the short wheelbase, overall length was only 163.5 inches. The blunt-looking fastback carried a classic Colombo-designed 60-degree, 3-liter V-12 beneath its elongated hood.

As a result of the car's redesign, shorter overall length, reduced weight, and increased output—280 hp at 7,000 rpm versus 260 hp at 7,000 rpm for the "Tour de France"—the SWB 250 GT was faster and handled better than its predecessors, making it an even more daunting competitor. All of the cars were equipped with four-speed synchromesh gearboxes and later models were offered with electric overdrive. The 250 GT SWB Berlinetta was also the first GT Ferrari sold with disc brakes. The hit of the Paris salon, order books were soon full, much to the frustration of would-be owners who were given no delivery date if their names were not known to be directly related to racing!

The body, designed by Pininfarina, was produced for Ferrari by Scaglietti in Modena. In creating a design to fit the shortened wheelbase, Pininfarina used no quarter windows, adding to the car's aggressive and shortened appearance. Most of the bodies were steel, with aluminum doors, hood, and trunk lid, although a few all-aluminum SWB bodies were built to order for competition. Pininfarina manufactured certain components for the steel-bodied cars while the doors, hoods, and deck lids were constructed at Scaglietti.

Special racing versions of the 250 GT SWB, with either all-alloy, or steel-and-alloy bodies, could be equipped with a larger fuel tank, necessitating relocation of the spare tire directly under the rear window. Additionally, a few 250 GT SWB Competition were built with tuned, 300 hp Testa Rossa engines with six carburetors.

When introduced, the 250 GT SWB was a contemporary to the Aston Martin DB 2/4 MK III, the Jaguar XK-150 S, Maserati 3500, Mercedes-Benz 300SL, and the Chevrolet Corvette. As a road car, it was without peer, and in competition, the 250 GTs quickly ran up a string of victories throughout Europe. In 1960, SWB Berlinettas won the Tourist Trophy race, the Tour de France, and the 1,000 km of Paris at Montlhéry. And in 1961, Stirling Moss, driving Rob Walker's SWB, won the Tourist Trophy for Ferrari a second time. In fact, during 1961 so many class wins were collected by SWB Berlinettas that when the season came to a close, Ferrari owned the GT class in the Constructor's Championship.

With a top speed of around 150 mph, the 250 GT SWB Berlinetta was one of the fastest sports cars of its time, a driver's car with nimble handling and superb balance, that allowed it to be driven hard into corners as well as flat out on a straight-away. It was, as one driver wrote, "... so easy and comfortable to drive fast, and so sure footed." The 250 GT SWB, in either lusso or competition version, wrote Hans Tanner, "... more than any Ferrari before or since, was a car equally at home on a race track or a boulevard." There were fewer than 200 examples built from late 1959 until early 1963.

Throughout Ferrari's early history, the road from Maranello was paved with cars like the SWB Berlinetta. Road cars that could go racing, and race cars that could go touring.

According to factory notes, a few steel-bodied cars were built with the oversized competition fuel-filler cap in the left rear fender, a trait normally restricted to the light-weight cars where it was located in the upper left corner of the rear deck, as pictured.

Chapter Three

Grand Touring
The Elegant Ferrari

Word association. Ferrari? *Red.* Ferrari? *Fast.* Ferrari? *Luxury car.* Excuse me. *Luxury car?* That's how history has interpreted the 1964 Ferrari 500 Superfast and its predecessor, the 400 Superamerica, sports cars that were afforded an extra measure of interior luxury and comfort and thus distinguished from the more traditional race-bred road cars. The luxury gran turismo theme, however, is firmly rooted in the late-1950s, when Ferrari introduced the 410 Superamerica.

Aside from pure race cars, every Ferrari road car of the 1950s was luxurious for its time. There was, however, what many customers perceived to be a compromise in Ferrari's road-going coupes and berlinettas, which were tied more closely to the company's racing heritage than to the luxury and comfort one found in early postwar Alfa Romeo road cars, for example. This was a point Luigi Chinetti continually brought to Enzo Ferrari's attention, a bone of contention that seemed to have these men at odds throughout most of the 1960s.

Minor styling changes by Pininfarina to update the Spyder California included reshaping of the rear fenders to reduce their width, a new rear deck, and new one-piece taillights.

The move to lusso styling, luxurious in an American context as Ferrari saw it, didn't come until the Pininfarina 250 GT 2+2 arrived in 1961. By the end of 1963 more than 950 had been delivered. For Ferrari these were phenomenal numbers.

Back in 1957, Ferrari had commenced series production of its first convertibles, the 250 GT Cabriolet. The first example, designed by Pininfarina, was shown at the 1957 Geneva auto show. The Cabriolets were not intended for competition, although with a 240-hp Colombo V-12 under the hood, there wasn't much aside from suspension, tuning, and a very plush interior that separated the car from its racing brethren. It was, perhaps, the ideal compromise between the two extremes.

The cabriolet's chassis was identical to that of the Boano coupes being produced at the same time using a welded oval tubular steel ladder-type frame with independent front and live rear axle and drum brakes.

A handsome if not stunning design, the early cars were noted for their dramatic grille, protruding Perspex-covered headlamps faired into the fenderlines, and bold vertical front bumperettes. The Pininfarina design featured a prominent air intake laid almost flat and extending nearly three-quarters of the hood's length.

The Spyder California's dashboard configuration and finish was virtually identical to the earlier Pininfarina Cabriolet Series I cars. The Spyder California was not as luxuriously upholstered as the Cabriolets and had more purposeful interior trim. Some cars were delivered to special order with more luxurious interiors, while others were provided minimal trim for competition. The cars used a four-speed all-synchromesh transmission with direct drive in fourth.

This, along with the headlight and bumper design, gave the car an aggressive appearance from the front. The first series cars were limited to approximately two dozen examples, all of similar design, while later versions (another 12 cars produced in 1958-1959) featured a one-piece wraparound front bumper and less dramatic uncovered headlights pushed farther out to the corners, giving the front end more of a squared-off appearance. It is estimated that Series I production ran to around 40 examples, all with steel bodies by Pininfarina.

Despite the roadworthiness of the 250 GT Cabriolet, Luigi Chinetti was looking for a more aggressively styled GT convertible to sell. Chinetti's was not the only voice beckoning Ferrari to send Pininfarina back to the drawing board and his engineers to task on a revised chassis and suspension. Ferrari's West Coast distributor, John von Neumann, also agreed with Chinetti that the 250 GT Cabriolet was not the kind of Ferrari his customers wanted. Von Neumann felt that an open car with the characteristics of the lighter berlinettas would be very popular in the United States. Il Commendatore complied and gave approval for a special series to be built, the 250 GT Spyder California, which went into limited production in May 1958 and was built through 1960 on the long wheelbase GT Berlinetta chassis.

The revised coachwork, penned by Pininfarina, was manufactured at Modena in the workshops of Scaglietti. The cars were produced in two series, the long wheelbase, of which less than 50 were built, and the short wheelbase, a lighter weight, steel and aluminum-bodied version introduced in 1960 and built through 1963. Again, around 50 examples were built.

The 250 GT Spyder California SWB was equipped with the 60-degree V-12 rated at 280 horsepower at 7,000 rpm. As with the majority of 250 GTs, carburetion was by three Weber twin-choke downdraft carburetors.

The Pininfarina Cabriolet was a striking design built on the long wheelbase 102.3-inch 250 GT chassis. The body lines featured the pronounced rear fender kickup first shown on the prototype 410 Superamerica in 1956.

An even sportier version of the Spyder California, the short-wheelbase model, was built on the same chassis as the 250 GT SWB Berlinetta, measuring 7.9 inches less in wheelbase than the first series Spyder California. The SWB cars had essentially the same handling characteristics as the competition-bred berlinettas, and like the first series spyders, were genuine sports cars.

Among a handful that were pressed into competition was one entered by Luigi Chinetti's North American Racing Team (NART) and driven by Bob Grossman and Ferdinand Tavano to a fifth overall finish in the 1959 24 Hours of Le Mans. Several California Spyders were also fitted with competition engines, and upon special order supplied with all-aluminum bodies. The cars were normally made of steel with aluminum doors and deck lids.

The LWB Spyder California was produced in three series. About seven cars were built before the new LWB 250 GT Berlinetta engine and chassis were used. It is estimated that 27 second series cars were produced between the end of 1958 and the end of 1959. Most of the competition versions came out of this production run. The third series cars were fitted with the outside-plug V-12 engine, developed from the 250 Testa Rossa and equipped for the first time with disc brakes. Pininfarina's minor styling changes to update the cars included reshaping of the rear fenders to reduce their width, a new rear deck, and new one-piece taillights.

The SWB Spyder California made its debut at the Geneva Salon in March 1960. These examples were equipped with new heads and larger valves, increasing output by 20 hp to 280 hp at 7,000 rpm. (Competition engines were further increased to 300 hp with even larger valves, high-lift camshafts, and lighter-weight connecting rods and pistons.) The track was widened on SWB models, which were also the first to

switch from lever-type shock absorbers to adjustable telescopic units.

The Spyder California, in either wheelbase, was one of the first Ferrari "driver's cars," a car that was capable of exceptional speed and handling, yet comfortable and luxurious enough for daily driving. The last example (4167 GT) was sold in the United States in February 1963. Total production of the Spyder California in all versions was 47 long-wheelbase and 57 short-wheelbase models.

At the same time Scaglietti was turning out Spyder Californias, Ferrari took steps to further differentiate the Cabriolet model, introducing the Series II in 1959. This model was built concurrently with the Spyder California through 1962. Still on the long wheelbase, the Series II Cabriolet was even more of a boulevardier than the Series I with styling similar to the Pininfarina coupe, sans roof. It proved to be one of the most luxurious open Ferraris of the era.

Luxury via Maranello never looked better than it did in the next great Ferrari road car, the 250 GT Berlinetta Lusso, a breathtaking stretch of automobile

The engine in the 250 GT Cabriolet Series I was a Colombo-designed 60-degree V-12 with a bore and stroke of 73x58.8 mm (2.870x2.315 inches) displacing 2,953cc (180ci). The valve operation was by a single overhead camshaft on each bank with roller followers and rocker arms to inclined valves. With three twin-choke Weber carburetors and a compression ratio of 8.5:1, output was 240 hp at 7,000 rpm.

The 250 GT Cabriolet interior was plush for a Ferrari, with leather upholstered seating, console, door and kick panels, and a dashboard finished in a glare resistant matte black crinkle texture.

Chassis number 1803, this is the first 250 GT SWB Spyder California produced. Chassis specifications for the SWB were almost identical to those of the SWB Berlinetta. With a wheelbase of only 94.5 inches and lighter overall weight than the LWB Spyder California, the 1960–1963 models were the best handling of the series and the most attractively styled. The covered headlights of the early production cars were later abandoned, and the headlamp configuration changed slightly to accommodate chromed bezels. In general, this early design is considered better looking.

that even today rivals Ferrari's best efforts. Production of this model totaled only 350 from its introduction at the Paris Auto Show in October 1962 until the last body left Scaglietti in 1964.

The Lusso was the most daring new design from Pininfarina since the 410 Superamerica. With styling that resembled a touring version of the 250 GTO, the 250 GT Berlinetta Lusso is considered by many to be Pininfarina's greatest design for Ferrari.

With the Lusso, Sergio Pininfarina and his staff had delivered the first contemporary Ferrari road car of the 1960s. The Lusso body was a series of graceful curves, from the front fenders to the upturned rear spoiler, and free of any superfluous chrome trim to embellish its shape. Prunet described the new design as Pininfarina's escape from the "cubist" period, which had prevailed throughout most of the 250 GT and 410

SA models. The Lusso actually capitalized on many of those earlier designs. The forward-projected head-lamps integrated in the fenders were straight off the Series I Pininfarina Cabriolet. Even the bumper design drew its shape from the bumperettes of the early cabri-olet. Where the Lusso departed from past designs was in the rear fender treatment, which began at the wind-shield posts and carried all the way back through the tops of the doors until they met with the edge of the abbreviated deck lid—the only flat plane on the entire car. The design of the Lusso, noted Prunet, was all in accord with the aerodynamic theories of Dr. Professor Wunibald Kamm of the Stuttgart Techical University and proven by Pininfarina and Ferrari on the 250 GTO.

The Lusso's shape, which pioneered the aerody-namic vogue of the 1960s, was complemented by an interior that was the most luxurious in Ferrari history.

Not as powerful as other 250 GTs, the Lusso's V-12 delivered 250 hp at 7,000 rpm, some 30 hp less than the 250 GT SWB Berlinetta.

Within the roomy cabin, driver and passenger snugged into true bucket-type seats, upholstered in hand-sewn leather. The speedometer and tachometer were housed in two large pods in the center of the dashboard, with small secondary instruments behind the steering wheel. This feature was unique to the Lusso. There was also a full luggage shelf behind the seats, as well as a modest trunk, making this the first Ferrari road car that could carry enough luggage to actually take on the road.

Aside from exemplary styling and interior design, the 250 GT Berlinetta Lusso was also the fastest sports car of its day with a top speed of 150 mph at 7,400 rpm.

When the last Lusso pulled away from Maranello at the end of 1964, it marked the conclusion of the 250 GT era. Over a period of 10 years, the 250 GT designation was applied to nearly 2,500 Ferraris.

Although the engine and chassis of the 250 GT Berlinetta Lusso were pretty much standard Ferrari fare, the body design was Pininfarina's greatest design achievement of the 1960s. The Lusso was a genuine GT; as such, it was not well insulated, so engine noise (hardly a negative characteristic when it is a Ferrari V-12) filled the cockpit, making conversation difficult. Dean Batchelor noted that most of the noise was due to the low rear-axle gearing (high ratio), which caused the Lusso's V-12 to run at higher rpm.

The Lusso interior was unique to this model with a distinctive, if not unusual, placement of the primary gauges in the center of the dashboard. This, perhaps, gave the passenger an opportunity to note exactly how fast the car was going! For its time, the Lusso interior was plush with a great deal of attention paid to leather trim and carpeting. The dashboard was upholstered in a nonreflective black leather, lending both a luxurious and functional touch.

In profile, the Lusso displayed its stunning fenderlines flowing from the headlights through to the truncated rear deck lid. The Lusso's styling pioneered the aerodynamic vogue of the 1960s and inspired a number of subsequent designs, particularly the rear aspect which appeared again on the new 275 GTB. One interesting characteristic is the narrow width of the rear pillar, which gives the car a wraparound window effect and virtually no blind spot. During its two-year production run, approximately 350 Lussos were built.

The 330 GTC was an astounding combination of three Ferrari body styles, using elements from the 400 Superamerica, 500 Superfast, and 275 GTS. "A combination that could have been a disaster," as Ferrari historian Dean Batchelor once noted. Instead, the 330 GTC turned into one of Ferrari's most attractive two-place coupes. Although popular in Europe, sales of the 330 GTC were not exceptional in the United States. American buyers were looking for more aggressively styled and more powerful sports cars. Approximately 600 examples of the Ferrari 330 GTC were produced through the end of 1968.

While the Lusso had come closer to being a true touring car than any of its predecessors, Ferrari had already undertaken development of a genuine luxury model with the 400 Superamerica, which was built concurrently with the Lusso through 1964. The 400 Superamerica was also designed by Pininfarina, drawing on several auto show styling themes from the early 1960s, including the sensational Superfast II shown at the Turin motor show in 1960. The 400 Superamerica gave rise to the 500 Superamerica in 1964.

Essentially, Pininfarina had retained the aesthetic style of the aerodynamic coupes, but refined and tailored the lines of the 500 Superfast more closely to that of the 250 GT Berlinetta Lusso, which had been a styling triumph for Ferrari.

The 500 Superfast made its debut at the Geneva Motor Show in March 1964. It was a larger, more luxurious and more powerful replacement for the 400 Superamerica. Under the hood was a Colombo-based, 60-degree V-12, unique to the 500 Superfast. For this model, displacement was increased from the Superamerica's 3,967cc to 4,962cc (302.7ci). This was accomplished by using the 108-mm (4.26-inch) bore centers of the 1950 Lampredi-designed long-block 60-degree V-12 together with the general mechanical layout of the big Colombo V-12, thus creating a hybrid engine with an 88-mm (3.46-inch) bore and 68-mm (2.68-inch) stroke.

In 1964 the 500 Superfast had the most powerful engine available in a passenger car. The first series, about 25 examples, used the same four-speed, all-synchromesh transmission with electrically operated overdrive as the 400 Superamerica. The second series, an even dozen cars, built from late-1965 to the end of production in 1966, were little changed but did include new side louvers in the fenders and a new five-speed all-synchromesh gearbox, with direct drive in fourth gear.

The Superfast was built on a 104.2-inch wheelbase (50 mm longer than the 400 Superamerica LWB platform) with a 55.5-inch front and 55.2-inch rear track, both slightly wider than the 400. The suspension was of similar design: A-arms, coil springs, telescopic shock absorbers in front, and a live axle rear with semi-elliptic springs and telescopic shock absorbers. Other than the engine, mechanical specifi-

The 500 Superfast interior was the most luxurious of any Ferrari built up to that time with the use of wood veneers to accent the instrument panel and center console.

The engine of the 500 Superfast was unique to the car. It was effectively an extended Colombo engine with the same 108-mm spacing between the bore centers as the long-block Lampredi, but with removable heads. The 500 Superfast could attain a top speed of 174 mph.

cations for the 500 Superfast were almost identical to the companion 330 GT introduced in 1964.

The 500 Superfast was the most luxurious car Ferrari had built up to that time. The ultimate in front-engined Ferraris "for those who like the Rolls-Royce touch with their performance," as historian Hans Tanner wrote in 1974. But no one summed up the Super-

america better than Antoine Prunet who decreed that "Ferrari and Pininfarina had, without question, created quite well the Ferrari 'Royale.'"

Maranello's flagship coupe was luxuriously upholstered in buttery leather and accented with hand-rubbed wood trim on the instrument panel, dashboard, and center console. Power windows were a standard feature as was an AM/FM push-button radio.

Ferrari's advances in the field of luxury GTs reached an all-time high for the 1960s with the introduction of the 330 GTC and GTS models in 1966. Shown at Geneva in March, the 330 GTC was the ultimate Ferrari hybrid utilizing the chassis of the 275 GTB, the engine of the 330 GT 2+2 (introduced in 1964), and a body design by Pininfarina that combined the aerodynamic styling of the 400 Superamerica and 500 Superfast with the 275 GTS. As Dean Batchelor once noted, "a combination that could have been a disaster. . . ." However, in the skilled hands of Pininfarina, the juxtaposition of design elements from two berlinettas and a spyder turned into an extraordinarily attractive coupe.

A truly modern Ferrari for the times, it featured four-wheel fully independent suspension with unequal-length A-arms, coil springs, and telescopic shock absorbers, disc brakes on all four wheels, and a five-speed, all-synchromesh transmission built in-unit with the differential to deliver 300 hp from the Colombo-based V-12.

The 330 GTC was closer than any model had come to combining the power of a Ferrari V-12 with the unadulterated luxury of a touring car. It was fast, comfortable, and quiet. You could even have air conditioning.

Being all things to all people has always been a difficult task, but Ferrari made one remarkable overture to that end with the 330 GTC. Production lasted from mid-1966 to the end of 1968, at which time the engine was enlarged to 4.4 liters and the car was renamed the 365 GTC. This version was continued through 1969.

As Ferrari prepared to enter the 1970s, an entirely new line of road and competition cars was under development—cars that would once again break new ground in design, performance, and enineering.

The 330 GTC used the same engine as the earlier 330 GT 2+2, a 300-hp Colombo-based V-12 displacing 3,967 cc (242 ci). The cars were equipped with a five-speed, all-synchromesh transmission built in-unit with the differential.

A rear deck design traditional of Ferrari spyders such as the 330 GTS adapted surprising well to the coupe configuration of the 330 GTC, which actually preceded the 330 Spyder into production by six months.

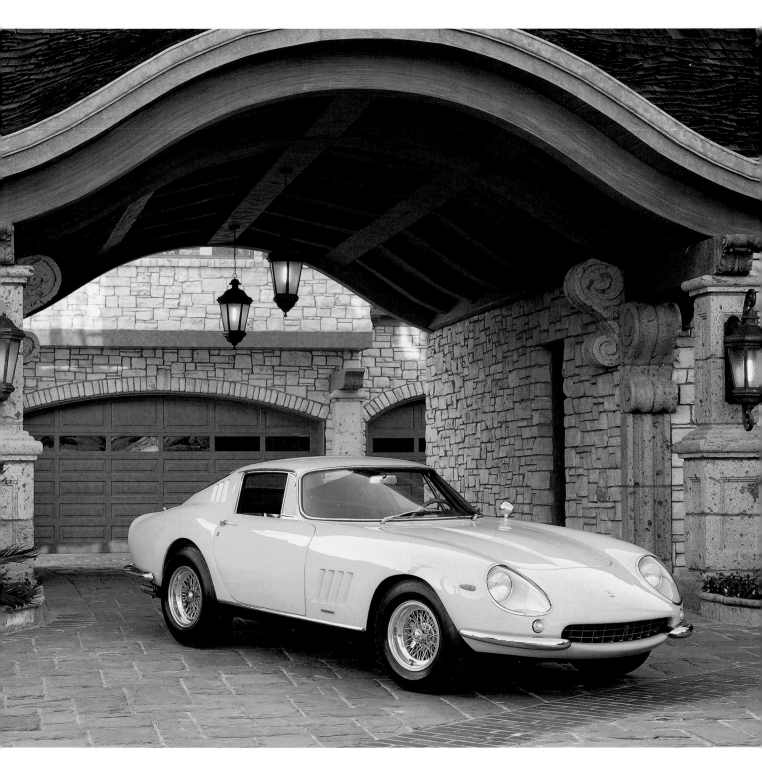

Chapter Four

Ferraris for All Seasons
The Great Road Cars

The most charismatic road car to come from Maranello after the 250 GT Berlinetta Lusso was the all-new 275 GTB. Originally introduced as a two-cam model in 1964, it was the first of Ferrari's now legendary 1960s-era Berlinettas offered to customers in touring or racing configurations.

Customers had the option of three Weber carburetors (with which the GTB was homologated for competition by the FIA) or a phalanx of six Weber 40 DCN/3s, endowing the engine with a brake horsepower capacity approaching 300. There was also a choice of construction offering a combination of steel and aluminum or all-alloy bodywork. Stylish Campagnolo 14-inch cast alloy wheels, recreating the design used on the 1963 Typo 156 Formula 1 cars, were standard, with the traditional Borrani wire wheels offered as an option.

Dean Batchelor noted in his *Illustrated Ferrari Buyer's Guide*, "The 275 series marked the progressive change in Ferrari design philosophy from thinly dis-

guised racers to comfortable and luxurious transportation vehicles. Because of the chassis changes—primarily the four-wheel independent suspension—the 275s were not only faster, but more comfortable than their predecessors."

Equipped with the Colombo-designed 60-degree V-12 displacing 3,286cc (77x58.8-mm bore and stroke) and dispensing 280 hp at 7,600 rpm with the triple Webers, the 275 GTB was the ultimate expression of Ferrari's ideology, a road car suitable for racing that gave up little, if anything, to purebred competition models. With that in mind, Ferrari also offered a limited number of 275 GTB/C models (about a dozen) stripped for out-and-out racing, equipped with a dry-sumped engine and lighter-weight sheet metal bodywork. Exactly two years after the introduction of the 275 GTB, the four-cam version made its world debut at the Paris Auto Show.

Ferrari was seldom first to introduce technical innovations. After all, Jaguar had been offering a double overhead cam (dohc) engine in its production and competition cars since the late 1940s. Over the same period, Ferrari had been content to offer a single overhead cam (sohc) engine (albeit a V-12) until the early 1960s. By that time, more and more European road

The car that led to the development of the 365 GTB/4, the Pininfarina-designed 275 GTB/4 Berlinetta. With the introduction of the Daytona, Ferrari bid farewell to the famous oval grille and fender-mounted headlight design that had been a hallmark since the late 1940s.

The 275 GTB/4 engine was another Colombo-based 60-degree V-12 design using double overhead camshafts on each bank. Compression ratio was 9.2:1 with fuel delivered by six Weber twin-choke downdraft carburetors. Output for the four-cam was rated at 300 hp at 8,000 rpm.

cars were appearing with four-cam engines beneath their hoods. Not only Jaguar, but Aston Martin, and in Italy, Alfa Romeo, Maserati, and a new Italian marque, Lamborghini. Enzo was more or less being enticed into the dohc market by his competition. If he was going to join in the fray, however, it would be on his terms.

The 275 GTB four-cam was derived from the 3.3- and 4-liter engines which had powered the 275 and 330 P2 prototypes of the 1965 racing season, engines which were themselves derivatives of Colombo designs dating as far back as 1957. Change, but not for the sake of change. It is interesting to note that between the first Ferrari 12-cylinder 125 model of 1947 and the 275 GTB of 1964, that is to say over a 17-year career, Ferrari's 60-degree V-12 engine had gained more than 140 percent in specific power! Never before had Ferrari offered such a competition-oriented road car to the public: double overhead cams, dry sump lubrication, six twin-throat Weber carburetors, and 300 hp at 8,000 rpm.

The new four-cam engine was introduced in a revised 275 GTB body at the October 1966 Paris Auto Show. The prototype GTB/4, with chassis number 8769 GT and engine 8769 GT, was designed by Pininfarina and built (as were nearly all 275 GT bodies) by Scaglietti.

Sergio Pininfarina's exotic styling for the 275 GTB and GTB/4 captured with great success the better elements of the competition-built 250 GTO, as well as, at the rear, the styling of the GTB Lusso. Pininfarina's approach was the perfect *leitmotif* for the new Berlinetta—a long, plunging hood, small oval radiator intake, streamlined covered headlights, pronounced hood bulge, truncated rear, and fastback roofline all perfectly harmonized to the contour of the steeply inclined and sharply curved windshield. The 275 GTB/4 was nothing short of aesthetic classicism, and if the car had any detractors, their only protest was that it too closely resembled the GTO. Hardly a fault.

The GTB/4 proved an incomparable dual-purpose sports car that could challenge the ability of even the most skilled drivers. Commented author Stanley Nowak, in his book, *Ferrari—Forty Years On the Road*, "Like all of the best Ferraris, driving [the GTB/4] automatically focused one's concentration on getting the most out of it. It responded in kind. The more one puts into it, the more one gets out of it. Like most Ferraris, it is intended for serious drivers." Says veteran race driver Phil Hill, "It was like a boulevard version of the GTO."

While there are enthusiasts who will argue the point, the majority will agree that the 275 GTB and GTB/4 were the best-looking berlinettas ever produced by Ferrari. Of the four-cam models, only about 280 examples were built. The rarest of all 275 GTB/4 models, however, were those *not* produced by Ferrari. At least, not directly.

Back in 1952, Luigi Chinetti had established Ferrari sales outlets in both Paris and New York City, where his showroom was located on the west side of Manhattan. His international racing exploits from Le Mans to the Carrera Panamericana had made him famous among sports car cognoscenti and granted him entrée into European and American café society. Luigi Chinetti was to Ferrari what Max Hoffman was

The styling of the 275 GTB and GTB/4 was an evolution of the 250 GTO and GT Berlinetta Lusso, the influences of which can be seen in this rear three-quarter view.

to Porsche—the conduit through which great cars would pass into the hands of racing and sports car enthusiasts of means.

When Chinetti decided to abandon the driver's seat in his late 50s, he had won at Montlhéry—Ferrari's first postwar victory in 1948—Le Mans in 1949, a second 12-Hours at Montlhéry with co-driver Jean Lucas, and the Carrera Panamericana with Piero Taruffi in 1951. He had also become a prominent figure in U.S. sports car racing, having placed cars in the hands of friends like Bill Spear and Jim Kimberly, who contributed to Ferrari's growing popularity in North America. However, it was Chinetti's involve-

ment in developing two of Ferrari's most celebrated models, the 250 GT Spyder California and the 275 GTS/4 NART Spyder, that made him legendary among Ferraristi.

In his memoirs, *My Terrible Joys*, Enzo Ferrari barely mentioned Chinetti's name, yet without him, it's unlikely Enzo Ferrari would have had much to write about. History will remember Chinetti, who succumbed to a heart ailment in 1994, shortly after celebrating his 93rd birthday, as the man who truly built the Ferrari legend.

As a dealer and importer, Chinetti understood the American market, perhaps better than Hoffman. To

Within the production run of 275 GTB and 275 GTB/4 models, there were short-nose and long-nose versions, a slightly larger rear window, and exposed trunk hinges. The car pictured is the actual 1966 prototype built by Pininfarina and displayed by Ferrari at the 1966 Paris Auto Show.

The 275 GTB had been the first Ferrari road car to offer four-wheel independent suspension. The GTB/4 would be the first equipped with a dohc engine. Not what you could call a significant change in the model, at least from appearances, but from behind the wheel, the GTB/4 had a character that clearly set it apart from its sohc predecessor. Although it looked nearly identical, except for a prominent hood bulge, the GTB/4 offered owners a 300-hp dohc V-12.

please his customers, Luigi would not only challenge Ferrari's decisions, but at times he would go out on his own and have special Ferrari models produced at his own expense.

By the mid-1950s, he had moved the Ferrari dealership from Manhattan to Greenwich, Connecticut, where he formed the North American Racing Team, better known as NART, in 1956. It was to be an independent arm of Scuderia Ferrari, that on occasion would also represent the factory when Ferrari decided not to enter events under his own name. Over the years, NART became one of the most illustrious acronyms in American motorsports and a virtual who's who of legendary race drivers. Among those who drove for or were discovered by Chinetti were Mario Andretti, Dan Gurney, Masten Gregory, Pedro and Ricardo Rodriguez, Paul O'Shea, Richie Ginther, Phil Hill, Stirling Moss, Bob Bondurant, Sam Posey, Jim Kimberly, Brian Redman, and Denise McCluggage.

The 275 GTB chassis, with a wheelbase of just 94.5 inches, was a proven design of ladder-type welded tubes with a four-wheel independent suspension consisting of unequal-length A-arms, coil springs, and telescopic shock absorbers.

Over the 26-year period between 1956 and 1982, NART campaigned in more than 200 races with more than 150 different drivers.

Because of their friendship, Il Commendatore had granted Chinetti the right to use the Cavallino emblem as part of the NART insignia. However, all the decisions regarding the team were Chinetti's, and he found himself at odds with Ferrari. They were two very stubborn men heading at times in the same direction, and at others, quite the opposite way. They were, as former race driver and author Denise McCluggage once put it, "indeed similar. Similar in the way that Yin and Yang are similar. You know, like hills and valleys; you can't have one without the other."

Recalls McCluggage, who knew both men very well, "Luigi was more like the director, the *auteur* . . . always behind the scenes, while Ferrari was always grandiose, the grand figure."

Next
Several GTBs were modified for racing by their owners, but Ferrari also addressed competition with the 265 GTB/C or GTB Competition, which was offered in the spring of 1966. While the GTB/C retained the general appearance of the GTB—from the exterior, the only obvious difference between the two was larger wheels and slightly flared wheelwells—mechanically the differences were really quite radical. Ferrari produced 12 275 GTB Competition cars between May and August 1966.

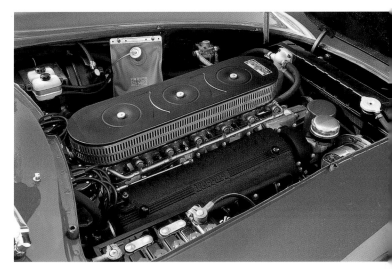

The 275 GTB/C engine had high-lift camshafts, 250 LM valves, reinforced pistons, a special crankshaft, and new Weber 40 DFI 3 carburetors. Built solely as a competition car, the GTB/C was equipped with a dry sump engine lubrication system with a separate oil reservoir.

The 275 GTB and GTB/C had two immense gauges—speedometer to the left and tachometer to the right—set into a wide oval instrument pod. Oil pressure and temperature gauges were positioned in between. The remaining instruments and switches were distributed across the center of the dashboard, practical in layout, yet accomplished with an elegant flair and just a hint of chrome embellishment.

155

The Other Ferrari Road Car: The 206GT Dino

The Dino is very much a part of the Ferrari road car legend, even though, technically, it is not a Ferrari, since the engines were built by Fiat.

In a very loose interpretation, the Dino was to Ferrari what the 914 was to Porsche, a less-expensive companion model. To Enzo Ferrari, however, the reasons for producing the Dino were very personal. The high-performance V-6 models were produced to commemorate Il Commendatore's son, Dino, who had died in 1956.

Dino Ferrari had suffered from muscular dystrophy since birth, but had much of his father's will. He managed to get through school and acquire a degree in engineering, but as his health began to fail, he was forced to spend most of his time in bed. Enzo and his close friend Vittorio Jano,

The Dino design by Pininfarina was one of the most curvaceous bodies ever produced for a sports car, a fact that contributed to the car's longevity. The cars bore no Ferrari emblems (the *cavallino* was added by a dealer), and the only reference was the Dino GT name next to the taillights and the Pininfarina body plate forward of the rear wheelwell. The cars were built on a 92.1-inch-wheelbase welded tubular-steel frame with four-wheel independent suspension and disc brakes. Only the 206GTs were bodied in aluminum.

one of Italy's greatest automotive engineers, would spend time with Dino in his room discussing the young Ferrari's ideas for a 1.5-liter racing engine. Dino had even written a two-part article on the design of a V-6 high-performance engine in the Italian magazine, *Velocita*.

Writing about Dino in his memoirs, Enzo Ferrari said that, "For reasons of mechanical efficiency [Dino] had finally come to the conclusion that the engine should be a V6 and we accepted his decision." Five months after Dino died, Ferrari created the 156 Dino engine.

Dino's inevitable death still came as a blow to Enzo. To honor his memory, Ferrari developed an entire line of Dino engines over a 10-year period for Formula 1, Formula 2, sports racing, and GT road cars.

Pinifarina bodied the first Dino road car to be powered by a rear-mounted V-6 eingine. The prototype known as the Dino 206GT Speciale was displayed at the Paris Motor Show in October 1965. A second version called the Dino Berlinetta GT was displayed at the 1966 Turin Motor Show, and like the earlier example, the engine was positioned longitudinally ahead of the rear axle. A third and final version made its debut at Turin in November 1967, this one with the Fiat-produced engine mounted transversely and built in-unit with a five-speed transaxle. An additional prototype was shown in Brussels the following year and early in 1969 production started at Scaglietti. By the end of the year roughly 150 Dinos had been built, all with aluminum bodies.

The 206GT was the first production Ferrari to be given only even chassis numbers (road cars had, with few exceptions, been serialized in odd number only) and the first not to wear either the Cavallino emblem or Ferrari name. It simply bore the signature "Dino GT" on the right corner of the body below the engine cover.

The majority of first series Dinos were sold in Italy and Europe, although a few were brought into the United States by Luigi Chinetti in 1969. The 206GT was replaced in 1969 by the 246GT, which remained in production through 1973. The 246GTS, featuring a removable targa-type roof panel, was added in 1972 and concluded Dino production in 1974.

The engine in the first Dino model, the 206GT, was a 180-hp, 65-degree V-6 displacing 1,987cc with a bore and stroke of 86x57 mm. The subsequent Dino engines used in the 246GT and GTS displaced 2,418cc with a 92.5x60-mm bore and stroke and increased output to 195 hp at 7,600 rpm.

The development of the NART Spyder in 1967 was the culmination to one of their most famous disagreements. To Luigi, spyders and convertibles were not interchangeable designs. Each had a well-defined purpose. When Chinetti had been a race driver, spyders were open competition models like the 166 MM, cars that had no windows or top, whereas a convertible had a folding top and wind-up windows. The fact that the differences were becoming less defined was the reason he had pressed Ferrari to build the 250 GT Spyder California in 1958 and then the SWB version in 1960.

By 1964, the Ferrari production car line had been divided into four models. First the lavish 500 Superfast, continuing the luxury image Ferrari had established in the early 1960s with the 410 and 400 Superamericas, then the sleek 330 GT 2+2, and the stunning 275 GTB and GTB/C Berlinettas. At the end of the line was the passionless 275 GTS, a spyder in name only,

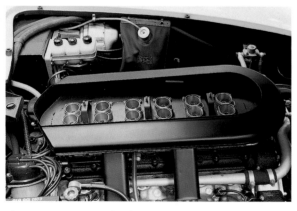

The Type 226 V-12 used in the NART was based upon the P2 prototype racing engines that had been used by the factory team in 1965. The dual overhead camshafts were an obvious design change from the previous 3.3-liter GTB. The revised V-12 delivered up to 330 hp at 8,000 rpm and breathed through six Weber 40 DCN 17 carburetors, which are shown here.

built atop the GTB platform but with an entirely different body design. In appearance it was a much more conservative styling concept that retained none of the GTB's exquisite lines. To Chinetti, calling the 275 GTS a spyder was a sheer corruption of the word, and in terms of its spirit and intent, an unworthy replacement for the Spyder California.

Since Ferrari had little interest in building a new spyder for the American market, Chinetti's course was clear. His son, Luigi "Coco" Chinetti, Jr., had proposed to build a spyder based on the new 275 GTB/4 Berlinetta, arguably, the car Maranello should have produced instead of the ignoble 275 GTS. To accomplish this, they turned to Sergio Scaglietti, commissioning the carrozzeria to build a series of Competition Spyders exclusively for Chinetti Motors and NART. Scaglietti was an artist when it came to converting berlinettas into spyders, and what emerged from the Modena coachbuilder's palette was a hand-built masterpiece.

Chinetti had selected the greatest Ferrari of its time as the basis for the NART Spyder. Equipped with a four-cam V-12 breathing through six Weber 40 DCN 17 carburetors and delivering up to 330 hp at 8,000 rpm, the 275 GTB/4 was built atop a revised Type 596 all-independently suspended chassis, with the engine, prop-shaft tube and transaxle all rigidly mounted along the frame, as on the new Ferrari 330 GTC.

From the exterior, the four-cam model was easily distinguished from the standard 275 GTB by a raised central power bulge in the hood. It was also obvious whenever a driver applied substantial pressure to the throttle pedal—the GTB/4 could move from rest to 60 mph in 6.7 sec and reach a top speed in excess of 150 mph.

The rebodied berlinettas were delivered by Scaglietti to Chinetti Motors in Greenwich and sold in North America. Although Maranello scarcely acknowledged the existence of the 275 GTB/4 NART Spyder, it was to become one of Ferrari's most sought-after models.

The first car arrived stateside in February 1967. Stamped with chassis number 09437, it was painted Giallo Solare (sun yellow) and contrasted with a rich black leather interior. Enzo Ferrari did not believe that yellow was a proper color for a competition car bearing

Redesigning the stunning 275 GTB/4 Berlinetta into a Spyder was a task few would have undertaken, but Sergio Scaglietti took the Pininfarina fastback and cut the roof cleanly away leaving the same flowing rear fenderline intact and blending it perfectly into the rear deck lid.

his name. "ProBoBly," said Chinetti in his Italian-accented English, "the scorers do not miss yellow so easily." Ferrari simply replied, "You have made a taxi cab." And so one more little battle of wills had been fought by these two giants; Ferrari, the car maker, and Chinetti, the image maker.

Following the 1967 Sebring race, Chinetti gave the car a complete overhaul and a new paint job—this time a deep burgundy—and sent it off to *Road & Track* magazine for testing. The article appearing in the September 1967 issue reported an impressive top speed of 155 mph, and it ran 99 mph duringa 14.7-second standing-start 1/4-mile. *R&T* proclaimed it, "the most satisfying sports car in the world." After the road test, the car was delivered to the movie set of Steve McQueen's new film *The Thomas Crown Affair*. Although only briefly featured in the 1968 thriller, McQueen, an impassioned

The interior of the NART Spyder was straightforward in Ferrari tradition, no superfluous trim, just the necessary instruments and a hand-sewn leather dashboard. Seats were upholstered in black leather. The color scheme was a vivid contrast to the soft yellow exterior of the first car. Note the large metal-gated shifter used on the 275 series.

Above and Below

The first of their kind, the 1968 Ferrari 365 GTB/4 Berlinetta and 1969 Ferrari 365 GTS/4 Spyder prototypes. Both cars featured the Perspex nose band with concealed headlights, a stunning design that was not permitted in the United States. The prototype Daytona Spyder pictured (serial number 12851) was the only example built with the Perspex-covered European headlights. Any other Spyders with such covers were either retrofitted by the owner or the entire car converted from a European Berlinetta to a Spyder, a not too uncommon practice in the 1980s.

sports car enthusiast and accomplished race driver, was so taken with the NART Spyder that he purchased car 10453 from Chinetti.

Although nine examples hardly constitutes production, among Ferraris it is a respectable number, especially for a car that the factory had no intention of building. Thanks to Luigi Chinetti's vision of a proper spyder, today we have the 275 GTS/4, a car in which we can all delight until a time when such things as automobiles no longer matter and the world no longer resonates to the sounds of 12-cylinder engines.

The 275 GTB/4 Berlinetta and Spyder became the most recognized and desirable Ferrari models of their time, albeit, a very short time. Exactly two years after the four-cam prototype appeared on the Ferrari stand in Paris, the all-new 365 GTB/4 Daytona took its place.

"Berlinetta" and "spyder" are two of the most important words in the Ferrari language, words that define the essence of the automobile before one knows the year or model. So it was to be with the 365 GTB/4, which for many Ferrari collectors has become the ultimate example of the differing design strategies.

The Ferrari Daytona was first introduced in Europe as a Berlinetta in 1968 and then as a Spyder the following year. Displayed at the Paris Auto Salon, the prototype coupe was actually the third Daytona design created by Carrozzeria Pininfarina but the first to use the new 365 motor and to closely resemble the production car. Built on a 275 GTB chassis, every body panel and piece of glass was different from the later 365 GTB/4 production models, and the 1968 prototype was the only Daytona actually built by Pininfarina. The production cars were all produced for Ferrari by Scaglietti.

Since Ferrari first began offering road cars in the late 1940s, the Berlinetta design had evolved into one of Maranello's most popular body styles for both road and competition cars. Ferrari styling had for years dictated that every car have a dynamic grille, a pronounced, aggressive visage epitomized by such models as the 250 MM, 340 Mexico, and 250 GTO. For the Daytona, however, Sergio Pininfarina and his staff were about to take a detour, departing from all previous Ferrari models and abandoning for the first time the traditional oval grille that had become a Ferrari hallmark.

The Daytona's original design called for headlights concealed behind a clear plastic cover. The dynamic new design, however, was not in accordance with federal headlight height requirements, and the design had to be changed for export models. Ferrari found it necessary to design a second front end which positioned iodine headlamps in a retractable housing that mimicked the Perspex nose when the lights were off and "popped" up (Corvette style) when they were turned on. All models originally sold in the United States were so equipped.

Breaking from tradition was a difficult decision for Sergio Pininfarina. For more than a decade he had designed bodies for Ferrari that were imbued with a sense of heritage, and however different they may have been from model to model, there was always a distinctive look. The 250 GTO, 250 GTB Lusso, and 275 GTB had been the first cars to significantly advance aerodynamic design at Ferrari, but they still bore traditional Ferrari styling cues. Pininfarina was convinced that aerodynamics were now as important to the car's performance as the suspension and driveline.

Surrendering the aggressive oval grille design for the first time, the Daytona presented a sharp, thin line from the front, with the radiator intake forming a horizontal slit beneath the nose. In one bold stroke, Sergio Pininfarina had changed the Ferrari's formidable open mouth into a malevolent grin.

This new approach to front-end styling presented one unique challenge: where to place the headlights, which had for more than 20 years been a part of the fender design. With the 365 GTB/4, however, there were no front fenders, at least not in a classic sense. This brief

From fastback to flatback, the 365 GTB/4 Spyder's revised design featured a new deck lid and flush boot cover that blended perfectly into the body's curve. Compared with the Berlinetta, the Spyder was dramatically different. It appeared lower, even more virile than the coupe, and it was more fun to drive. Indeed, there was no substitute for the wind curling over the windshield and the aromas of the open road teasing around in the cockpit.

impasse led to the most dramatic styling change in Ferrari history—the elimination of faired-in headlamps.

For the 365 GTB/4, Pininfarina chose to set the headlamps back under clear rectangular covers, which blended with the line of the front deck. Small horizontal bumpers were set into either side of the radiator air intake, with small parking lights tucked in just above, and small, round marker lights positioned on each side of the front fenders. At least one prototype incorporating these changes was built in the late summer and early fall of 1968. On the final version, the paired headlamps were set slightly back from the nose of the car, but the entire nose was now covered by a single band of transparent plastic approximately eight inches high. This nose band wrapped around the front corners of the car to integrate parking and side marker light units, ending just short of the front wheel arches. Toward either end this plastic band was left essentially clear (there were fine white vertical lines on the inner surface) where it covered the four headlights. in the center, the inner surface of the perspex was painted black (still with fine white vertical lines), except for the very center which was left clear to display the rectangular Ferrari emblem attached to the bodywork underneath

There was much more to the 365 GTB/4 than its radical new headlight design, however. The hood was a highly complex series of curves and one of the most difficult pieces on the entire car. On either side and approximately halfway back there were two recessed air vents, located in a low-pressure area and serving as outlets for warm air passing through the combined water and oil radiator. Adding to the complexity of the hood, the trailing edge was curved to conform to the base of the windshield, with the gap between the hood and windshield varying from a mere fraction of an inch at the sides to several inches along the centerline of the hood. At the same time the plane of the hood bent sharply upward along the rear edge, giving the effect of a louver and in theory directing the airflow up to the windshield rather than bluntly into it.

The large gap created by the curve of the hood as it rounded the windshield served a dual purpose as an additional outlet for engine compartment air and a storage space to park the windshield wipers. In theory the wipers were supposed to be removed from the line of vision through the windshield, thereby precluding annoying reflections on the windshield, and by tucking them behind the louver at the rear of the hood, improving aerodynamics. Actually, the wipers had to be parked in view in order to clean the windshield.

A factory press release noted that the large, double-curved windshield had "an extremely aerodynamic line" and was sharply angled to the rear. It was attached to the body without a visible rubber gasket, which was recessed to improve the smoothness of the lines and covered by a thin strip of bright metal surrounding the windshield.

There was a decidedly rakish angle to the Daytona's roofline, establishing a fastback appearance at the rear of the body before angling down to the deck lid. An extremely large and almost flat rear window was used on the Berlinetta. It was installed in a manner similar to that of the windshield and also surrounded by a thin strip of brightwork. The tail section of the fastback was taken up with the rear deck lid, which ended along the rear edge of the upper bodywork on the prototype but extended down between the paired round taillights on production versions.

With only a few exceptions—most notably the 1962 250 GT Lusso—Ferrari Berlinettas were notorious for restricted rear vision. The Daytona would not follow suit. In designing the 365 GTB/4, Pininfarina used taller side windows extending upward from the beltline to the flat roofline, allowing drivers improved over-the-shoulder visibility. The door glass featured front vent windows on each side and aft of the door glasses, in the rear sail panels, were rear-quarter windows, followed in turn by a set of crescent-shaped air outlet vents, which were painted black. The entire window ensemble was surrounded by bright thin metal frames and an additional piece of brightwork along the drip molding above the windows to accent the roofline. The large expanses of glass helped lighten the visual effect of the rear half of the car as well as provide good visibility for the driver.

In keeping with Pininfarina's decision to eliminate unnecessary embellishments, the trim around the windows was just about the only evidence of brightwork. Even conventional door handles were eliminated. Instead, small levers swiveled out parallel to the bottom of the door windows, almost looking like part of the window trim. On the rear center of each door there was a small key lock, and that was all Pininfarina allowed to impair the smooth flow of the body lines.

One of the most significant styling characteristics of the 365 GTB/4 was the "trough-line", a concave molding used to create a visual divide between the upper and lower body panels, without resorting to the use of chrome trim. Fully encircling three-fourths of the car, it extended the length of the body from behind the front wheel arches to those at the rear and then around the back of the body above the bumpers. The sides of the Daytona were also somewhat narrowed in appearance by the sharp inward slant of the rocker panels giving the car an almost barrel-sided roll between the wheel arches.

Filling the void left earlier in the year by the discontinued 275 GTB/4 Berlinetta, the all-new Daytona made an immediate splash when introduced at the Paris Salon. However, it was not immediately available, and Ferrari did not produce the cars in any great number until the last half of 1969. Although it was the first Ferrari to be built in quantity to meet the U.S. regulations, the European version was marketed first and the U.S.-legal cars were not available on a regular basis until mid-1970; real quantities did not arrive until early 1972, when the new U.S. Ferrari importers took over. In the eastern United States a partnership was formed by the Chinettis and Al Garthwaite. In the West, the importer was Modern Classic Motors in Reno, Nevada, owned by renowned car collector and casino owner Bill Harrah.

In all probability the 365 GTB/4 shown in Paris was the final Pininfarina prototype finished in a bright Ferrari racing red with a red-and-black interior. The prototype built on chassis 11795 stayed with the factory until it was sold to one of its Formula 1 drivers, Arturo Merzario, in December 1970. That car is currently in a private collection.

Interior of the Spyder was identical to that of the 365 GTB/4 Berlinetta.

Ironically, the car's most attractive feature, the Perspex-covered headlights, became its greatest handicap when Ferrari tried to sell the Daytonas stateside. The plastic-covered headlights were not in accordance with federal height requirements. Ferrari found it necessary to design a second front end for export which positioned iodine headlamps in a retractable housing that mimicked the Perspex nose when the lights were off and "popped" up (Corvette style) when they were turned on, at which point the entire aerodynamic theory of the Daytona's front end design went out the window. So much for artistic solutions!

The body of the new car was not the only innovation. In order to meet new Federal emissions regulations that took effect in the United States in 1968, Ferrari's engineers had to come up with an efficient, clean-burning engine. The 365 GTB/4 model designation followed the Ferrari custom of stating the displacement of a single cylinder, followed by a set of letters and numerals that further defined the car. Thus, the new berlinetta had 365cc per cylinder (precisely 4,390.35cc total displacement), was a Gran Turismo Berlinetta, and had an engine with four camshafts.

The new 60-degree, dohc V-12 was derived from earlier designs by Gioacchino Colombo and Aurelio Lampredi. Displacing 4.4 liters (268ci) and teamed with six Weber DCN20 twin-barrel 40-mm downdraft carburetors, the fed-legal Ferrari engine delivered 352 hp at 7,500 rpm, taking the drive through a ZF all-synchromesh five-speed transaxle built in-unit with the differential.

Following the 275 GTB/4, the Daytona had a four-wheel independent suspension comprised of unequal length A-arms with tubular shock absorbers, coil springs, and front and rear antiroll bars. The Daytonas were also equipped with Dunlop ventilated disc brakes on all four wheels.

Underneath, a welded tubular steel ladder frame supported the car's 94.5-inch wheelbase and wider-than-normal 56.6-inch front and rear track. The Berlinetta's broad stance was contrasted by an overall length of 174.2 inches.

At the time of its introduction in 1968, the 365 GTB/4 Berlinetta was the most expensive and fastest road car in Ferrari's 21-year history. Priced at just under $20,000, the Daytona was capable of reaching a top speed of 174 mph, according to the factory. *Road & Track* recorded 0 to 60 in 5.9 sec and a top speed of 173 mph, but who's quibbling?

Following the successful introduction of the Daytona Berlinetta, work began on a spyder version to be introduced in 1969. Although building spyders was something of a tradition with Ferrari, beheading the 365 GTB/4 flew in the face of reason.

Designed to take advantage of Europe's high-speed autoroutes, the Daytona was the most aerodynamic model in Ferrari's stable. Pininfarina claimed that the outline of the body had been developed, both in general lines and in many smaller details, in accordance with studies conducted in the wind tunnel at the Turin Polytechnic Institute. Aerodynamics was as much a part of the car's performance as the refined V-12 engine under the hood. If the roof was removed, the aerodynamic gains were gone with the wind! Making a Daytona Spyder was not logical. Of course, who said logic has anything to do with automobiles?

"In Europe, we are accustomed to thinking of a sports car as a berlinetta. On the contrary, a sports car for an American many times means a spyder," says Sergio Pininfarina.

In total, 1,383 Daytonas were produced, including 122 spyders, 96 of which were sold to customers in the United States.

Chapter Five

Contemporary Ferraris
Road Cars of the 1980s and 1990s

Racing has been the foundation for nearly all of Maranello's advancements in the design of road cars. One of the most significant was the development of the Boxer engine in 1964.

Ferrari's first flat, opposed (180-degree V-12) Boxer engine was a 12-cylinder, 1.5-liter Formula 1 engine with 11:1 compression ratio, Lucas fuel-injection, and output of 210 hp at 11,000 rpm.

The Boxer name was derived from the piston's reciprocating movement, back and forth, toward and away from each other, like two boxers sparring. The term, however, was actually of German origin, used to describe the layout of the early Porsche and Volkswagen four-cylinder engines, which were also of flat opposed design.

The 365 GT4 Berlinetta Boxer—Ferrari's first midengine production sports car (discounting the Dino) was fitted with a 4.4-liter production version of the competition engine in 1974. Mounted behind the driver and ahead of the rear axle, it delivered 380 hp at 7,200 rpm.

Pininfarina's penchant for displaying the Ferrari engine reached an all-time high with the F40. The transparent plastic engine cover gave everyone a clear look at the inner workings of this incredible sports car.

The 365 GT4 BB would be the first of an entire generation of new rear-engined 12-cylinder models that would remain in production for more than 20 years. The main body structure of the 365 GT4 was steel, with the hood, doors, and rear deck lid made of aluminum and the lower body panels constructed of fiberglass. As usual, the design was by Pininfarina with the actual body production handled by Scaglietti in Modena.

The cars used the latest Ferrari suspension technology, with unequal-length A-arms, coil springs, tubular shock absorbers, and antiroll bars front and rear.

In a review of the 365 GT4 BB, Dean Batchelor noted, "Handling is great for the enthusiast driver. The steering, which is heavy at low speeds, lightens up as speed increases and the tail heavy weight distribution (43/57 percent), which would normally cause oversteer, is offset by a suspension with understeer designed into it—resulting in an agile, maneuverable car."

The 365 GT4 BB was the first Ferrari road car in many years to actually give drivers a taste of what a race car felt like. Ferrari produced the car until late in 1976, when the 512 Berlinetta Boxer took its place. The body styling of the 512 was almost identical to that of its predecessor. Pininfarina's revised styling added a "chin spoiler," or air dam, beneath the egg-crate front grille

One of Ferrari's longest-lived road cars was a true boulevardier; the 400GT was introduced in 1976 and was succeeded by the 400i GT in 1979 and the 412 in 1985. These were the first full-size 2+2 luxury touring Ferraris to be equipped with automatic transmissions.

and air ducts on the lower body sides forward of the rear wheels. Other changes included the now-famous 512 BB taillight array, with two large round lenses per side, reprised on the 1995 Ferrari F 512 M.

The 512 BB employed the same blended media construction as the 365 GT4 BB, using steel for the main body structure; aluminum for the hood, doors, and engine cover; and glass fiber for the lower body panels. The use of glass fiber led to the most distinctive and memorable styling characteristic of both the 365 and 512: a solid division line between the upper and lower body panels. On the 365 the lower part was always painted matte black. The two-tone color scheme was also available as an option on the 512 BB.

Displacement of the Forghieri-based 180-degree V-12 engine used in the 512 BB was enlarged to 4,942 cc (up from 4,390 cc in the 365) by a bore increase of 1 mm to 87 mm, and an increase in the stroke of 7 mm to 78 mm. While output from the

revised Boxer engine was actually decreased by 5.2 percent (down from 380 hp to 360 hp), peak horsepower was reached at 6,200 revs instead of 7,200. An interesting trade-off.

Both the 365 and 512 Boxers were raced by private entrants, but their time in the sun was brief and the racing effort short-lived. It was by far, however, the best road car Ferrari had brought to market up to that time. Batchelor wrote of the 512 BB, "The Boxers are fantastic cars to drive, with little *raison d'être* other than the sheer pleasure of driving the ultimate sporting GT car." Almost 20 years after its introduction, the 512 BB with its razor-edged styling and incomparable midengine layout remains one of the most desirable of all Ferraris. A car that still looks like it's going 200 mph while standing still.

Evolution in design has led to many of Ferrari's most outstanding and best-loved road cars, but none became more ubiquitous than the 308 GTB and GTS,

For a car that was closer to a race car than a road car in performance and handling, the 512 BB provided driver and occupant with an exceptionally high level of interior comfort and trim.

the most recognized Ferrari model ever produced, thanks in part to the television series *Magnum P.I.*, starring Tom Selleck. But moreover, Ferrari enthusiasts found this the most practical driver in Ferrari's history.

Pininfarina stylists combined the best attributes of the 246 Dino and 365 GT Berlinetta Boxer in the 308's design. Suspension was all independent in the then-traditional Ferrari layout, and the cars were powered by a four-cam, 90-degree V-8 engine mounted transversely just ahead of the rear axle. The 308 offered a spirited 255 hp at 7,700 rpm, and drove through a five-speed transmission. An open version of the 308, with a removable roof section similar to that used on

Beneath Pininfarina's sculpted deck lid was an equally attractive engine. The Forghieri-based, opposed flat-12 was designed to look as impressive as it felt under full throttle.

the 246 Dino and Porsche 911 Targa, was added to the line in 1977.

The longest-running model in Ferrari history, the 308, continued on into the 1980s in improved versions, the 308GTBi, 308GTB Qv (quattrovalve), and 328 Berlinetta and Spyder.

Back in 1987, when Ferrari celebrated its fortieth anniversary, Modena introduced the F40. The name was chosen to commemorate the production of Ferrari automobiles from 1947 to 1987, but the F40 was no badge-engineered commemorative issue. It was the first Ferrari since the 512 BB that was closer to a race car than a road car. It was also the least-practical Ferrari ever produced. Although, in the spirit of the original sports cars built in Modena 40 years earlier, the F40 was the ideal model to honor Ferrari's anniversary year. A sports car pure and simple.

The body was a Kevlar, carbon-composite shell surrounding a tubular steel Kevlar and carbon-composite framework, to which Ferrari had fitted a 478-hp, twin turbocharged dohc four-valve V-8 engine and a highly articulated four-wheel independent suspension. Little more was needed to take an F40 into competition than some additional safety equipment and numbers on the doors.

A recessed latch released the light-weight doors, allowing the driver to climb or drop, depending upon one's style or build, into the contoured racing seat. Getting into or out of the F40 became a learned art. Until one mastered ingress and egress, bruised hips and shoulders were constant companions.

For the $250,000 originally asked by the factory (prices approached $1 million as speculators bought and resold cars throughout the late 1980s), buyers received a great deal of sensory gratification with the F40, but little else. The interior had a full complement of gauges, everything the driver needed to know, and nothing more. No 12-way power-adjustable seats with driver memory. No power windows or accessories.

The styling of the 512 Berlinetta Boxer was taken directly from the 365 GT4 BB and updated by designer Sergio Pininfarina with the addition of an under-grille spoiler, which squared up the front end, and NACA ducts on the lower body sides forward of the wheel openings.

Previous
Last of the 308-derived V-8 sports cars, the Ferrari 328GT
Berlinetta and Spyder carried the same body lines in both the
European and American versions. The only substantial
difference was in horsepower, 260 for North America, 270 for
the rest of the world.

Virtually no interior trim, not even door panels or
door handles, you just pulled the cable slung in the
hollow of the door and it unlatched. And no radio.
Had there been one, it would have required a 300-watt
system to boost the volume over the engine because
the F40 had virtually no interior soundproofing. Even
if it had, who needed music? The deep bass exhaust
note under throttle, the treble whine of the V-8, and
the rhythm of the Pirelli P Zeros beneath you were a
symphony for the senses.

The F40 was pretty simple. You stepped on the gas
pedal, the car went fast, very fast; you hit the brakes, it
stopped; turned the wheel and it went where you point-
ed. Just the way Enzo Ferrari intended things to be.

The career of the flat 12 hadn't ended with the 512
BB (1976 to 1981) and 512 BBi (1981-1984). The design
was continued in the next generation of Ferrari road
cars, which began in 1985 with the all-new Testarossa.

In the fall of 1984, Ferrari unveiled the Testarossa
in Modena on the site of the original Scuderia Ferrari
facility in the heart of town. The name Testarossa,
which means redhead, was taken from one of Ferrari's
most legendary race cars, the 250 Testa Rossa, which
had rampaged across Europe in the late 1950s. And
like its namesake, the 1985 Testarossa was a radical
departure from conventional Ferrari designs. Pininfarina had pulled out all the stops, taking form and
function to a new level by essentially designing the
body around the engine, a 4,942-cc flat 12 delivering

The 40th anniversary Ferrari, the F40, became one of the most
speculative models in Ferrari history. At a suggested retail price
of $250,000, the limited-edition cars soared to nearly
$1 million as speculators and investors traded them like
commodities until the sports car market crashed. Says Ferrari
S.p.A Chairman and CEO Luca Cordero Di Montezemolo, "I
am personally very happy that the market went back to a
normal limit like it was in the early '80s because the last years,
in my opinion, were mad years and this is not good."

The 348 was the first two-seat convertible since the 365 GTB/4 Daytona Spyder, last sold in 1974, and also the first midengine two-seat Ferrari Spider ever. (Ferrari changed the spelling of Spyder with a "y" when referring to the Daytona, to an "i" when addressing later models.) The Spider was the evolution of the 348 tb/ts series announced in 1989. Power for the midengine 348 convertible was Ferrari's proven 90-degree light-alloy V-8. Displacing 3,405cc with an 85x75-mm bore and stroke, output from the four-valve per cylinder motor was rated at 312 hp at 7,200 rpm, and 228.6 ft-lb of torque at 4,000 rpm. The transmission is a transverse five-speed gearbox.

390 hp at 6,300 rpm in European trim and 380 hp in U.S. specification.

The most outstanding aspect of the design was the horizontal air intake strakes rending their way through the doors and into the rear fenders. This became the car's most distinctive characteristic and one that has never been successfully duplicated, except by Ferrari in the Testarossa's two succeeding models, the 512 TR and F 512 M.

The F 512 M was a glorious revival of the 1991 512 TR, itself a generation beyond the Ferrari Testarossa. The F 512 M also drew upon history for its name, resurrected from the 512 Berlinetta Boxer. This car also had another historical imperative. It was to be the first interim Ferrari model in decades.

An improved version of the Testarossa, restyled by Pininfarina hard on the heels of the new F 355 Berlinetta and the 456 GT 2+2, the 1995 F 512 M was destined to be discontinued, and everyone knew it. This was a car that would be judged as few had. Not by the press, whose opinions are often taken too seriously, but by the very owners who would plunk down hard-earned lire for a car whose fate had already been sealed. The F 512 M was to be the end of the line for the Boxer engine. A line that concluded an 11-year run in 1996, when the F 512 M was officially replaced by the 1997 550 Maranello, the first front-engine Berlinetta since the 365 GTB/4 Daytona.

Without overdoing the technical analysis, one could say little of the original TR remained. Mechanically, the F 512 M was a generation beyond. The Formula 1-inspired Boxer design delivered a heart-pounding 440 hp at 6,750 rpm, a full 50 hp better than the old Testarossa and 12 more than the 512TR.

Previous
The F 355 has improved on the virtues of every Ferrari built over the past 50 years. It is the first of the new guard, a Ferrari for a new generation of prancing horse devotees.

With 367 ft-lb of torque at 5,500 rpm, the new F 512 M had no difficulty vanquishing either of its predecessors. Zero-to-60 was a scant 4.6 sec, and top speed just 4 mph short of 200.

From the exterior, the most striking visual change in the Pininfarina styling was the aggressive front, reminiscent of the F40 and tempered with a touch of the new 456 GT's graceful form in and around the grille.

The F 512 M was a lighter, more powerful, more agile, and better-built version of the Testarossa, still as impressive in appearance as the original, generously wide on the exterior and incomprehensibly narrow inside, a Coke bottle mounted on aluminum caps and propelled by a rocket-like V-12 that could snatch your breath away at full song and leave you wishing for legendary roads to challenge. Indeed, the F 512 M was an

The F 355, in either Berlinetta or Spider form, is the most powerful Ferrari ever produced with a naturally aspirated V-8 engine. Output from the 90-degree, 3.5-liter, 40-valve dohc V-8 is 375 hp at 8,250 rpm. Exhilarating performance is tempered by sophisticated computer-controlled, fully independent suspension, antilock disc brakes, and variable ratio power steering.

interesting way to bid farewell to both the Testarossa and the venerable Boxer engine.

Traditionally, Ferrari's new model introductions were held in Italy and throughout Europe before the cars were shown in the United States. No automobile, let alone a Ferrari, has ever been introduced to the world on a city street. Of course, Ferrari is no ordinary automobile and Rodeo Drive in Beverly Hills, California, no ordinary street.

On Saturday, February 27, 1993, the most famous stretch of pavement west of Wall Street was closed to traffic and lined from one end to the other (some three city blocks) with more than 125 Ferraris, dating from 1948 to 1993. It was without question one of the most singularly impressive displays of Ferraris ever assembled. All for the introduction of Ferrari's 348 Spider.

The public debut of the new Ferrari was conducted by designer Sergio Pininfarina and Ferrari S.p.A. chairman and CEO Luca Cordero Di Montezemolo, who told the crowd of spectators that Ferrari chose Beverly Hills and Rodeo Drive for the car's world introduction because California is very important to Ferrari. (California represents some 35 percent of Ferrari's American market.)

Designer Sergio Pininfarina says that creating a new design is not an easy task, "The fundamental problem that exists with any new design is always the same. Our cars have been the best or among the best in the world, the highest prestige for 50 years. Every new car then is a challenge, because each time we have to reaffirm that we are good enough to redesign a car which brings such satisfaction to the owner."

Considering all of the designs he has created for Ferrari over the past 46 years, Pininfarina says, "It is difficult to say which one is the best because there are so many different designs, so many different types of cars." He thinks for a moment and as a smile comes across his face he says, "Yes, there is the Superamerica, which used to be my father's car, this is something unique, a Ferrari between the Ferraris, something extremely refined, extremely good taste, extremely powerful," and with a hint of humor in his voice he adds, "extremely expensive. The Superamerica is a car which is very dear to my heart."

The F 355 Berlinetta and Spider have one of the most luxurious leather interiors ever designed for a Ferrari. A true driver's car, the layout is straightforward in design with the traditional Ferrari polished-steel shift gate.

The latest generation of Ferraris, beginning with the F40, have really become the signature cars for Sergio Pininfarina. "I have had the pleasure of meeting many people at the Concours, [Pininfarina is a judge each year at the Pebble Beach Concours d'Elegance] and they tell me that they own a new Ferrari, or an old one, and then they say, 'Thank you for what you have done.' There is no satisfaction in the world better to me than this."

His feelings about Ferrari, he says, are difficult to describe in Italian, impossible in English. "When I see all these red cars in the sunshine, I see one lifetime of work. In one way I feel very proud, and in another, very conscious of the importance of my position with Ferrari for the future."

That future has taken the form of the 456 GT 2+2, F 355 Berlinetta and Spider, and the F 50. With the debut of the 550 Maranello for 1997, and Ferrari has closed the circle giving the firm a new car in every V-8 and V-12 category from berlinetta and spider to GT 2+2, thus marking the beginning of Ferrari's second half-century. Cars, that however different from those built 50 years ago, still turn heads and set minds to dreaming.

Next
The Testarossa has become one of Ferrari's most successful models with a production run lasting from 1985 to 1996. From Testarossa, to 512 TR, to F 512 M, this body style is unsurpassed as the benchmark design of the 1980s.

The Testarossa's new flat-12 engine looked very much like the 512 BBi, but in fact was completely new and had no parts in common with its predecessor. Output from the 4942-cc, dohc, 48-valve engine was 390 hp at 6,300 rpm.

The 1995 Ferrari 456 GT 2+2 takes up where the 400i and 412 left off a decade earlier, offering Ferrari owners a luxurious four-passenger touring car built in the Ferrari tradition. The car features a clean-sheet-of-paper, 442-hp V-12, six-speed transmission, electronically actuated, fully independent suspension, and state-of-the-art traction control and antilock braking.

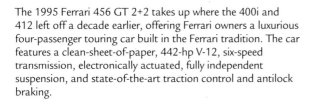

Track Testing Ferrari's Incredible F50

"HOW FAST?" The words blew back into my mouth as I tried to shout over the roar of wind surging past my head.

"ONE-SIXTY-FIVE!" Paul yelled. "I can do 180 on the next lap, but we'll have to go into turn one pretty hot. . . ."

"That's all right," I shouted, "I'll take your word for it. One-sixty-five is good enough."

Back in the pits, I realized that it wasn't the speed of the Ferrari F50 that had so impressed me—the car will break 200 mph if you give it enough room, but so will others—instead it was the undaunting way in which it tackled corners, as though inertia no longer had any relevance. More than the engine or body, it is the suspension that sets this Ferrari apart from other high-performance exotic sports cars. That, and a price of $480,000.

Few of Ferrari's vintage models can command that kind of money today, but after ever so little time in the F50 you understand why owners are willing to mortgage their souls to Modena for the privilege of leasing one.

"The lease," explains owner Paul Frame, "is Ferrari's way of preventing the market speculation that drove up the prices on F40s." Indeed, Ferrari is controlling the sale of the F50 by signing each owner to a two-year lease. "That's about $240,000 down and $5,500 a month," explains Frame. "Afterward, you have the option to buy the car for an additional $150,000." With owners locked into a two-year lease, there is little chance of speculators buying cars to resell. It is hoped the lease is worded to forbid subletting.

Money aside, this is the most remarkable nonracing car Ferrari has ever produced, although the line between race and road car in this case is so fine as to be almost imperceptible. The F50 is a street-legal Formula 1 car with a plush interior, as close to a purebred racer as any road car Modena has produced in the last half century. The F50 is the accumulation of 45 racing models and endless Granturismo and Sports models.

In theory, under the exotic Pininfarina-designed body, the F50 is a road-going adaptation of the 1990 Ferrari 641/2 Formula 1 car. It is built like a race car, around a central monocoque.

Made entirely of Cytec Aerospace carbon fiber, the F50 chassis weighs only 225 pounds and forms the central part of the car where the driver sits. Following Formula 1 design disciplines, the engine-gearbox-differential assembly is attached to the chassis with the engine anchoring the suspension, rear bumper, and bodywork elements. This is the first occasion that this system employing the engine as a structural element, as well as the propulsion medium, has been used on a street vehicle.

The F50's design places 43 percent of the car's weight on the front axles and 57 percent over the rear. To guarantee a tendency to understeer, the front track is 18 mm wider than the rear.

Prior to our track test, Frame ran the car at Texas World Speedway and attained 188.5 mph on the straight-away. "It's got really good gearing. The engine has a lot of torque in low rpm and one of the nice things about it is that it's streetable." Under 4,500 rpm the engine noise is muted. Get into the power over 4,500 revs and the F50 trumpets like a John Barry score. The engine actually changes temperament above 4,500 rpm and the two-stage induction system opens fully to double the volume of air being delivered. At the same time, the Motronic control unit reduces back pressure on the exhaust.

Frame admits that he hasn't really pushed the F50 that hard on the track. "I'm used to driving my F 355 Challenge

The styling of Ferrari's fiftieth anniversary model, the F50, is the most futuristic in the company's history. The Pininfarina body design is a road car adaptation of a Formula 1 race car.

When you settle into the driver's seat, you face an empty instrument pod until the power is switched on. Instrumentation is based on Formula 1 design and uses an 8-bit microprocessor that incorporates a downloadable event memory. The displays, which can only be seen by the driver, are LCD with 130 elements, transparency lit by electroluminescent bulbs. The major gauges in analog display are the tachometer and speedometer, which overlap each other so that redline appears almost to the immediate top left of the speedometer. A panel of tell-tales is positioned to the left of the tach, using ideograms to indicate various warnings. Fuel gauge, lighting indicators, and a digital clock are inset along the bottom edge of the instrument display. The dash is completely finished in suede to reduce glare in the highly curved windshield.

The heart of every Ferrari since day one has been the engine. Here Formula 1 regulations again played a role in the design of the F50's 286.7-ci V-12. The layout is a narrow vee of 65 degrees based on Ferrari's 1990 F1 car but increased in displacement from 3.5 liters to 4.7 liters. Utilizing four overhead camshafts and five vales per cylinder (three intake, two exhaust—a total of 60 valves in case you're counting), bore and stroke is 3.35x2.72 inches and compression a healthy 11.3:1. As rated by Ferrari, maximum horsepower is 513 at 8,500 rpm. Peak torque, 347 ft-lb, is delivered at 6,500 rpm. And with an overall weight of just 2,712 lb dry, the F50 carries around a mere 5.3 lb per horsepower.

Car on slicks, so when I'm on street tires with the F50 I'm just a little tentative." It's hard to think of 188.5 mph as "tentative." Frame has already gone through one set of the specially designed Fiorano tires. Named after Ferrari's test track, they were developed by Goodyear and are an impressive 245/35ZR18 front and 355/30ZR18 rear.

"There is some talk about manufacturing an F50 *competizione*. If they do that, I'm sure someone is going to make some slicks, and then I'll have an opportunity to see what the car can really do," says Frame. What it can do with the low-profile Fioranos is paste you into the seatback in a heartbeat. Zero-to-60 mph time is 3.7 seconds.

There is an unusually solid sound when the doors close, not the hollow thump you heard in the F40. The doors are upholstered and finely detailed. By comparison, the interior of the F50 is like a Rolls-Royce, and considerably more spacious than the F40's. Still, it is purely functional, the lower dash panel and most of the exposed interior surfaces are carbon fiber. The floor mats are rubber.

Racing-style seats using a composite frame are luxuriously upholstered in Connolly leather surrounding red fabric inserts for the seatback and cushion. The driver's seat and pedal rack are both adjustable to tailor the car to each owner.

With its clean, uncluttered interior layout, the most prominent feature is the center tunnel and shifter. The F50 gearbox is a wonderful blend of old and new. The high-tech carbon fiber shift knob and lever rest inches above a traditional polished-steel shift gate, linking the driver to a six-speed transmission with ZF twin cone synchronizers and a limited slip differential.

Technology at such a high price must come in an appropriate package, and Carrozzeria Pininfarina has pushed the envelope with the F50's styling. This is simply an outrageous-looking automobile. With the massive air ducts in the hood, wide oval grille, and integrated headlights, when seen head on, the F50 almost appears to be grinning. At nearly half a million dollars a copy, and with every one of the 349 cars to be built through 1997 already presold, someone certainly is.

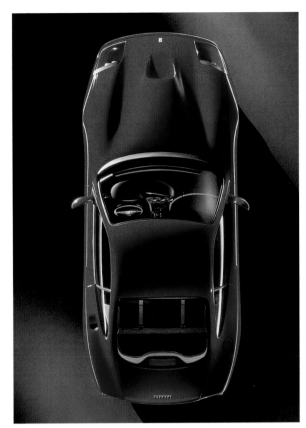

The 1997 550 Maranello replaces the F 512 M as Ferrari's performance flagship. The new SWB Berlinetta is the first front-engined V-12 since the 365 GTB/4 Daytona. It is built on a 98.4-inch wheelbase chassis and uses independent front and rear suspension with computer-controlled damping, as on the F50. A dual-mode ASR (traction control) system prevents wheel spin, although it can be switched off by the driver.

With the debut of a replacement for the F 512 M (Testarossa), Ferrari has closed the circle giving the firm a new car in every V-8 and V-12 category from Berlinetta and Spider to GT 2+2, thus marking the beginning of Ferrari's second half century.

PORSCHE

Randy Leffingwell

ACKNOWLEDGMENTS

My thanks for help in the production of this book go to Dick Barbour, San Diego, California; Jurgen Barth, Dr.Ing.h.c.F. Porsche AG., Weissach, Germany; Bob Cagle, San Diego, California; Bob Carlson, Porsche Cars North America, Reno, Nevada; Otis Chandler, Ojai, California; Tom Chang, Granada Hills, California; Warren Eads, Novato, California; Ernst Freiberger, EFA-Automobil Museum, Amerang, Germany; Fred Hampton, London, England; Ray Fulcher, San Juan Capistrano, California; Michael Hagen, Anaheim, California; Matt Harrington, Los Angeles, California; Dr. Warren Helgesen, Pasadena, California; Dr. William Jackson, Denver, Colorado; Dirk Layer, Vail, Colorado; Gerry Layer, San Diego, California; Michael Lederman, Parma, Italy; Robert Linton, New York City, New York; Jakob Maier, Amerang, Germany; Marco Marinello, Zurich, Switzerland; Kent Morgan, Arcadia, California; Dave Morse, Campbell, California; Kerry Morse, Tustin, California; John and Ray Paterek, Chatham, New Jersey; Helmut Pfeifhofer, Porsche Auto-Museum, Gmünd, Austria; Vasek Polak, Hermosa Beach, California; Jerry Reilly, Hardwick, Massachusetts; Peter Schneider, Dr.Ing.h.c.F.Porsche GmbH, Stuttgart-Zuffenhausen, Germany; Jerry Sewell, Newbury Park, California; Dick Simmons, Lake San Marcos, California; Paul Ernst Strähle, Schorndorf, Germany; Carl Thompson, Hermosa Beach, California; Bruce Trenery, Emeryville, California; and Derrick Walker, Warrington, Pennsylvania.

1948 Gmünd coupe **Holzmodel, opposite page**
Formed of ash, a holzmodel, or wood form model, of the Gmünd coupe sits outside the Porsche Auto-Museum in Gmünd, Austria. The original form was broken up and burned for winter heating long ago. Museum owner Helmut Pfeifhofer used original drawings to pattern his replica.

Chapter One

EARLY DAYS: PERFECTING THE FOUR-CYLINDER

On December 1, 1930, Dr. Ferdinand Porsche placed a bet on the rest of his life when he opened his own engineering and design firm. The Austrian-born engineer was fifty-five years old. He had spent thirty-five years employed by other companies, producing electric and gasoline engines and trucks and cars. His accomplishments and reputation were good enough that he felt confident of his future. He had come to consider industrial Stuttgart, Germany, as his home even though he was born in agricultural Zell am See, Austria. While he earned his engineering doctorate from Vienna Technical Institute, he had received an honorary doctorate from the Technical University in Stuttgart. Now, after several years with Austro-Daimler and Steyr, car makers in Vienna, he returned to Stuttgart to start his own company. His twenty-one-year-old son Ferry joined in the effort.

1955 Typ 550/1500RS Spyder, opposite page
Designed by Erwin Komenda, ninety of these aluminum-bodied racers were produced by Wendler Karosserie, and first examples appeared in August 1953. Ernst Fuhrmann's Carrera four-cam engine produced 100hp at 6200rpm, and was capable of propelling these 1,298lb two-seaters to 125mph.

To keep the work organized, Porsche numbered each job he undertook. Suspecting that no client would feel comfortable being a design/engineer's first project, he began his first commission, (a 2.0-liter car for the Wanderer company) and arbitrarily numbered it Typ 7. Work continued to come in. A Grand Prix race car for Auto Union was Typ 22. Later a 29ft long, six-wheeled Daimler-Benz land speed record attempt car was Typ 80.

Porsche's interest in affordable cars for the masses matched an ambition of Germany's leader, Adolph Hitler, for whom Porsche's design firm had already done other work. At the 1934 Berlin auto show, Hitler announced plans to introduce a "people's car", a *Volkswagen.* Porsche's firm was to produce three prototypes.

Prosperity led Porsche to move to suburban Zuffenhausen in June 1938. His staff numbered 176 workers designing, testing, and assembling automobiles. In 1940, Dr. Porsche

1948 Gmünd coupe Holzmodel, next page
The coupes were fabricated out of aluminum by a panel beater named Freidrich Weber working for Professor Ferdinand Porsche. The aluminum panels were bent and hammered into the contours of the wood form and then welded together.

1952 America Roadster
Stripped to bare metal following restoration prior to painting and reassembly, these aluminum panels gleam under bright lights. Porsche produced three series of America Roadsters, at the instigation of Viennese-transplant Johnny Von Neumann who had resettled in southern California. Von Neumann wanted a lightweight car to race and wanted a roadster body style because of climate. The bodies were fabricated by Heinrich Gläser Karosserie in Wieden-Ullersicht near Nuremberg.

received the honorary title of Professor, again from Stuttgart's Technical University.

Porsche created the Volkswagen in Zuffenhausen. Other government projects, including tanks and armored weapons, were born there as well. But the German military command could not protect the firm during Allied bombing raids. When the factory was damaged in April 1944, Porsche set out to save his company. While the headquarters stayed in Stuttgart, engineering, design, and assembly works went to Austria. Modest production began in a sawmill in Gmünd, 100 miles south of Vienna. When the war ended, Ferry Porsche moved to Gmünd.

Work done for the German government before the War came back to haunt Professor Porsche and his family. Porsche was first and foremost an engineering firm intent on staying in business; the government was one of few paying clients. The Professor, notoriously apolitical, refused to salute Germany's commander-in-chief and, to Hitler's continued annoyance, always referred to him only as Herr Hitler. Still all the men in the Porsche family, including his daughter Louise's husband Dr. Anton Piëch, were arrested by the French in mid-1945 and questioned about their activities. Ferry was released almost immediately but it was another two years before it became

1956 356A GS-Carrera

The Carrera's engine was introduced in the 550 Spyder racing cars and its name came from the Mexican road races that Porsche won in 1953 and 1954. But according to Engineer Ernst Fuhrmann, his Typ 547 twin-cam flat-four engine, his first design project, was meant not only to race but also to fit into his own high-speed road car.

1956 356A GS-Carrera
The Typ 356 body design was penned by Porsche's designer and friend Erwin Komenda. Its round compound curves set the style for every Porsche since. Referred to as an "organic shape," it has very few straight lines.

1956 Typ 356A "LeMans Coupe" replica, right
Oregonian Gary Emory created the "European" replica for his own amusement, even fitting a 2-liter 914 engine that was modified to resemble the Fuhrmann flat four. Porsche wore No. 45 at LeMans in 1953 on a Typ 550 coupe with louvered panels instead of rear windows.

1956 Typ 356A "LeMans Coupe" replica, opposite page
Born of a cannibalized 356A coupe, enough parts were missing from this car that its restorer enjoyed artistic license and recreated a Gmünd-style LeMans bodywork. Louvered side panels replaced the rear windows and were welded in place. Plexiglas duct work feeds air into the engine.

clear that the Porsches were engineers, not warriors, and they were released. Prior to that, Louise Piëch—who was running the 200-employee operations at Gmünd along with her brother Ferry—accepted a commission from Italian car maker Piero Dusio to design a Formula One Grand Prix racer for his Cisitalia firm. Porsche's concept used a water-cooled V-12 engine positioned behind the driver. The engine used dual overhead camshafts, a supercharger, and a five-speed transmission that could operate with four-wheel drive. The firm used Dusio's first payment to free Prof. Porsche and Dr. Piëch.

After two years in a cold prison in solitary confinement, Prof. Porsche, nearly seventy-two, was quite ill. When he returned to Gmünd, his primary goal was to produce a sports car bearing his name. At the Swiss Grand Prix in July 1948, the European press saw the first Porsche, a mid-engined, tubular space-frame car using mostly Volkswagen components. Hand assembled in Gmünd, the aluminum-bodied two-seat roadster, Typ 356-001, reached 85mph with a modified 1.1-liter VW engine.

Purely open cars were impractical for Europe. Through Dr. Anton Piëch, a Swiss hotel owner offered Porsche financial backing, and this allowed new design work and assembly to begin. The coupes that resulted, while still aluminum bodied, differed in configuration from the first roadster. The coupe's engine was placed behind the rear wheels to accommodate occasional passengers (or more luggage) behind the front seats. Ferry Porsche set a goal of producing 500 cars but its start was inauspicious; only four coupes were assembled in 1948. About sixty of these Gmünd coupes were completed by 1952.

Journalists loved the car. Its high price insured the coupe an exclusive audience appeal. Response at the 1950 auto shows hinted that sales would come. Porsche moved back to Stuttgart and arranged with Reutter Karosserie to build steel car bodies. When Prof. Porsche turned seventy-five in September 1950, more than 250 cars had been sold. When he died of a stroke in 1951, his car and his company were on their way. Three years later 5,000 Porsche Typ 356s had been sold.

In 1952 Porsches were offered with three engines, the wildest being a 1.5-liter overhead-valve version designed by a recently hired, young Viennese engineer, Ernst Fuhrmann. This engine could push the rounded coupes to 100mph. A year later fully-synchronized transmissions and larger diameter brakes were offered as well. A convertible followed.

Porsche encouraged racing. It recognized that stories in newspapers about the accomplishments of drivers like Austrian Otto Mathé and others created interest that Porsche could not afford in advertising. Enthusiasm spread throughout the world and took hold strongly in the United States.

1958 356A Cabriolet with hardtop
Porsche produced open cars, cabriolets, from its first models built in Gmünd, Austria. Soon after the company's move to Stuttgart, cabriolets began to appear from the factory in 1950–1951. Evolution occurred slowly and models improved steadily, with changes and upgrades incorporated continuously.

1958 356A Cabriolet with hardtop, above
The removable hardtop offered several benefits. It provided increased headroom, far superior weather sealing, and better rear visibility. It made the cabriolet into a true year-round convertible. The 356s offered other options including padded leather seats, a heater, sun visors, tachometer, carpeting and a variety of engines.

1958 356A Cabriolet with hardtop, left
Reutter Karosserie built the standard 356 cabriolet bodies in its factory right alongside the Porsche works in Zuffenhausen. (Eventually, this building was absorbed into the Porsche complex.) With the hardtop removed, the cabriolets reminded first time viewers of an inverted bathtub.

1958 356A Cabriolet with hardtop, above
The 356s were powered by 60hp 1600 Normal or 75hp Super engines. The 1600 Normal Cabriolet with hardtop sold new for about $4,250. Ernst Fuhrmann's 100hp Carrera engine was also available at a premium price. Carrera-GS cabriolets sold new for $5,260.

1958 Typ 718 RSK Formula 2, right
The first RSK appeared at the Nurburgring in May 1957, but versions with an optional center steering position for hill-climbs or FIA Formula 2 races did not exist until 1958. A handful were produced; two were used as factory team cars while the others were sold to privateers.

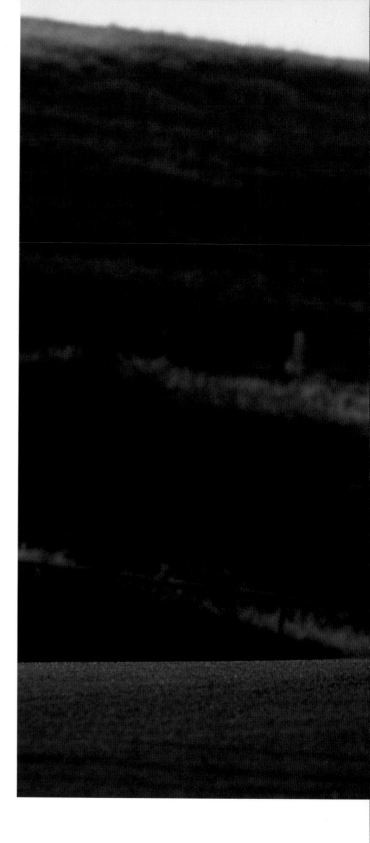

1958 Typ 718RSK Formula 2
The sleek Wendler aluminum bodies covered Ernst Fuhrmann's Typ 547/3 Carrera engine. Breathing through two Weber carburetors, the engine produced 142hp at 7500rpm. Weighing only 1,166lb, the cars easily reached 150mph. Conversion from left-side to center-steering took four hours.

Distributor Max Hoffman had brought Mercedes-Benz, Jaguar and other makes to the U.S. He saw Porsche as a new prospect for his customers. Hoffman's West Coast distributor Johnny Von Neumann was a racer first and salesman second. At Von Neumann's urging and Hoffman's pressure, Zuffenhausen produced a small run of sixteen aluminum-bodied America Roadsters in 1952. These were truly Porsche's first purpose-built racing cars. Victories by drivers like Jack McAfee, Ken Miles, and others, reported in American newspapers, did as much for Porsche in the U.S. as racing had done in Europe. Within another three years, as interest grew, Von Neumann visited Hoffman again.

Von Neumann wanted another open car—closed cars were too hot for California—but he wanted one for the streets to sell for $3,000. Von Neumann and Hoffman felt it was necessary to fight the price and performance competition offered by Triumph, Austin-Healey, and Jaguar. After Reutter slightly redesigned the roadster body and stripped every accessory from it, Porsche delivered its new low-slung Speedster for $2,995. They sold like mad. Owners paid extra for everything: tachometers, padded seats, floor mats, sun visors, cigarette lighters, heaters, and even clip-on hardtops. Produced from 1955 through 1959, Porsche sold more than 3,600 Speedsters. A docile 1500cc Normal 60hp engine was available. So was Ernst Fuhrmann's new four-cam Carrera-engined GS-GT package with 100hp. Not only did the name "Speedster" enter enthusiast jargon, but so did the car's shape, which resembled an overturned bathtub.

1960 356B 1600GTL Abarth Carrera
Only twenty-one of the Zagato designed, Abarth-built aluminum-bodied FIA Gran Turismo category competitors were assembled. Its looks defy its scale. It appears much longer than its 157in and much lower than its 52in height. German racer Paul Ernst Strähle made racing history many times in three different Abarth Carreras.

1960 356B 1600GTL Abarth Carrera
The Abarth's were fitted with the Typ 692/3A engines, with bore and stroke of 87.5x66mm for total displacement of 1,587cc. Carburetion was either Solex or Weber, and dual distributors were driven off the crankshaft. The twin-cam engines produced 135hp at 7300rpm.

The Fuhrmann Carrera engine (Typ 547) was introduced in 1953 for use in the Typ 550-1500RS racers, the Spyders. Throughout Europe and America, Spyders became the car to race if the racer wanted to win. In some events they made up almost the entire field. Spyders evolved into Typ 718s, the RSKs. The "K" came from the shape of a front suspension modification that proved unsuccessful. But the name persisted even though subsequent RS-60s and RS-61s reverted to a safer suspension configuration. Design improvements such as dual distributors and enormous Weber carburetors coaxed more than 150hp out of the flat-four Carrera. The 718s earned countless wins. Fitted with an optional center-steering position, these cars tantalized Porsche with the possibilities in international Formula Two and Formula One racing. In 1961, the beautiful Typ 804 introduced an extremely complicated flat-eight cylinder 1.5-liter engine designed by Hans Mezger. Sadly, it came up short of its competitors. Superb driving by teammates Dan Gurney and Jo Bonnier saved Porsche from humiliation, but the costs far exceeded the benefits, and Porsche withdrew from Formula One at the end of 1961. Other projects needed the resources.

As the fifties progressed, more luxury was offered for the road cars. Fitted luggage was optional, and a bench seat could be ordered, particularly on the 1955 U.S.-only model called the Continental. Lincoln protested the name, citing plans to reintroduce its own Continental in 1956. Initial U.S. exclusivity of the Speedster and Continental models miffed German buyers, and a "European" coupe model arrived in 1956.

1962 Typ 804 Formula 1
Successes in Formula 2 between 1958 and 1961 gave Porsche the courage to contest Formula 1 with this clean-lined single-purpose machine. Unfortunately, the effort was premature, the complex engine not yet powerful enough for competition. Its greatest victory was before a hometown crowd here at the Solitude Race Circuit in Stuttgart.

1962 Typ 804 Formula 1
The tiny cigar barely fit American racer Dan Gurney who recalled sticking out of it like a giraffe. It sat not quite 32in tall, barely 12ft long, and weighed only 1,010lb. Four were built, the second team car driven by Swede Jo Bonnier with a third car as team back up.

The 356A introduced in 1956 brought more modifications and improvements to the coupes and cabriolets. These all-steel bodies were fitted with a curved windshield. A gas gauge was standard equipment. Porsche reduced wheel size from 16in to 15in. In 1959, it offered a new convertible built by Drauz Karosserie in Heilbronn near Stuttgart. This Convertible D provided roll-up windows and a taller top than the Reutter Speedsters.

In late 1959, Porsche first showed the Model 356B, the T-5 body, that could be ordered with the new Super 90 engine. Then in 1961 the T-6 body was introduced; the windshield and rear window were larger, the front deck lid squared off to increase luggage capacity, and the fuel filler cap was removed to the fender. Owners could now refill the tank without opening the trunk. The Carrera 2 was introduced in September 1961. This 2-liter four-cam engine produced 130hp and had evolved from Ernst Fuhrmann's 1.5-liter Typ 547 as Porsche's most powerful street engine yet.

July 1963 brought the 356C with race-proven four-wheel disc brakes. Three engines were available, the 1600C, 1600SC, and the Carrera 2. A total of 450 of the Carrera 2s were sold, overlapping from 356Bs to Cs. Then two months later in September, the Typ 901 was shown at the Frankfurt Auto Show. This car introduced a new shape and the opposed-six-cylinder engine. The 356C and SC remained on sale through late 1965. Production of the Typ 901 began in late 1964, renumbered Typ 911 after Peugeot claimed its right to production car designations with "0" in the middle.

The Typ 901 was conceived in the late 1950s. Each iteration of the flat-four cylinder engine was thought to be its last and best. The 356's ten-year-old round shape contrasted with longer, swoopy Jaguars, Ferraris, and Corvettes. Still, sales of the organic-shaped cars held steady and Porsche hesitated to fix something that seemed unbroken.

1962 Typ 804 Formula 1
The magnificently complex Typ 753 flat eight-cylinder needed 195 to 200hp but, hard as engineer Hans Mezger worked, it never exceeded 180hp at 9200rpm. Formula 1 in those days had a 1.5-liter displacement limitation. The Typ 753 had a 66x54.6mm bore and stroke for a total of 1,494cc.

1964 356SC Cabriolet, previous page right
Beginning in 1963 with the introduction of the 356C models, four-wheel disc brakes, manufactured by ATE, were standard equipment, requiring different wheels. Otherwise the C-model cars were virtually identical to late production 356Bs (known as the T-6 bodies). Twin air-grilles were most noticeable. The 356B and C models brought the fuel tank filler outside to the passenger's front fender and enlarged the front trunk lid to improve access.

1964 356SC Cabriolet, above
Underneath the car, a slightly thicker anti-roll bar, along with slightly softer rear torsion bars, improved handling. Adjustable Koni shock absorbers were standard on SC models. The 356SC used Porsche's Typ 616/16 engine with twin Solex carburetors to produce 95hp at 5800rpm. The standard 1600C engine produced 75hp at 5200rpm.

1964 356SC Cabriolet

Recaro seats were a key element in Porsche comfort. In March 1964, Porsche acquired Reutter Carosserie, its neighboring coach builder. Seat production was retained by the newly formed Recaro group, a name formed from the first letters of each word. The 356SC interior comfort was further aided by improving heating, defrosting, and ventilation. The cabriolets were popular and over the final three years of production, from 1963 through 1964, more than 3,100 were produced.

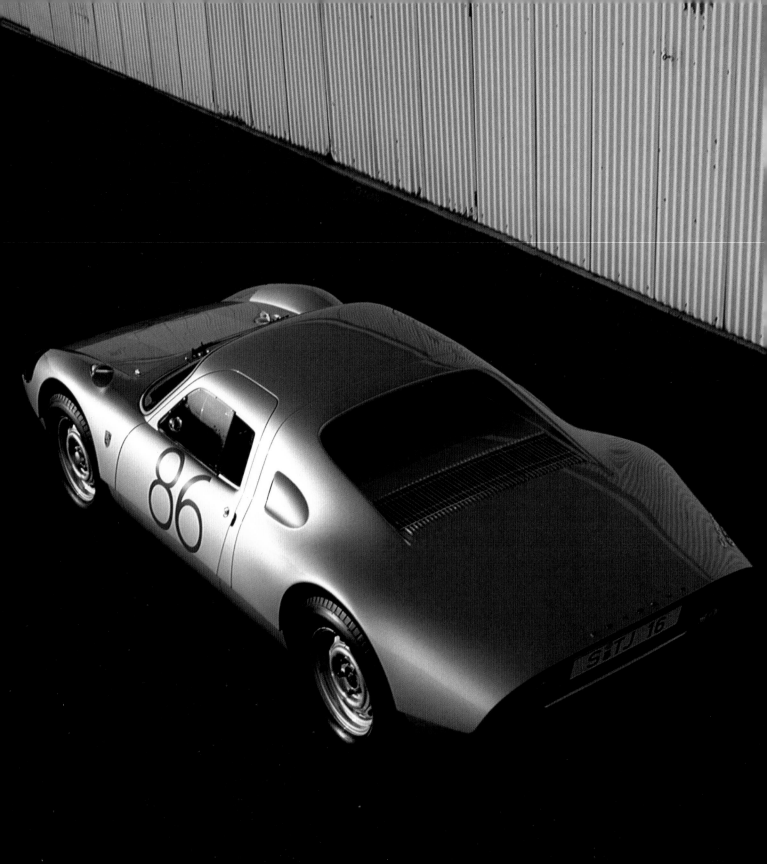

Chapter Two

BIGGER ENGINES, GREATER SUCCESSES

Ferdinand Alexander Porsche ("Butzi"), Ferry's twenty-eight-year old son, joined the firm in May 1957 and worked through his father's design education process. Butzi became head of a styling department of seven people in 1958. His education culminated in his forming the shapes of the 901 street car and Typ 904 Carrera GTS racing car. Using plasticine, a car modeler's clay-like material, he created the 904 on a tight deadline that allowed no changes. The production car was done on a more relaxed schedule.

Money no longer devoted to Formula One racing permitted further engineering developments in the 901 that improved steering geometry and suspension. Excluding some minor enhancements (engine air-intake vents were moved from the fenders to the rear deck lid), Butzi's original ideas hit showrooms nearly intact. Two models were offered. A four-cylin-

1964 Typ 904 Carrera GTS, opposite page
Many racers and designers regard the Carrera GTS as the most aesthetically pure race car design ever. Wearing No. 86, this car, 904-006, won the Targa Florio in April 1964, was twelfth at Nurburgring in May, and third in GT class at LeMans in June. In January 1965, it took second overall in the Monte Carlo Rally and launched Porsche's rally career.

der version using a detuned 356SC engine was called the 912 and was introduced in the U.S. for $4,690 while the 911 sold for $6,490. Half of the first year production was destined for the U.S. market.

Porsche's last four-cylinder 356SC cabriolets were sold in 1965. The need for a new open car model was apparent. Californian Johnny Von Neumann commissioned Italian designer Nuccio Bertone to produce a prototype. The new 911 chassis proved to be not stiff enough for a completely open car. Butzi Porsche's solution, announced in September 1965, was heralded as "The world's first safety convertible." Rather than disguise its integral roll-over bar, the Targa model—named to honor the Sicilian road race—emphasized it in brushed stainless steel. A roll-up canvas top and separate plastic window could be removed and stored in the trunk. By 1968, a hard rear window was available, the Sportomatic semi-automatic transmission was introduced, and several new interior and engine packages were offered. The 911T (touring), 911L (luxury) and 911S (sport) were introduced. (U.S. exhaust emission standards required modifications that delayed the 911S arrival until 1969.)

1964 Typ 904 Carrera GTS
It began as a question: could Porsche make an entire car in plastic? FIA's Group 3 offered possibilities, and in November 1962, parameters were set for the Typ *904. Working in Plasticine, a car modeler's clay, Butzi Porsche shaped the lines. Four months later the first prototype was driven.*

The 911L was discontinued in 1969 and the 912 went in 1970, to prepare for the arrival of the 914 mid-engine car. A fuel-injected Model 911E (Einspritzung—injection—in German) filled the middle range. It provided less luxury than the now-fuel-injected S model but gave comparable performance. A major handling improvement resulted from length-ening the wheelbase by 47mm—nearly two inches—behind the front seats.

From 1965 through 1969, Porsche racing achieved ever greater accomplishments. In 1965 Louise Piëch's son, twenty-nine-year old Ferdinand, was named head of engineering and development. For Piëch, outright overall victory was the only objective. Class

1964 Typ 904 Carrera GTS
*The no-frills interior left the fiberglass showing.
On early cars, the roll bar was not incorporated into
the fiberglass body and fit outside the back window
glass in notches in the rear bodywork. The entire
car weighed 1,433lb; it was capable of 0–60mph
in 5.5sec and, depending on gearing, more than
155mph at the top end.*

1964 Typ 904 Carrera GTS
*Development chief Hans Tomala planned the car to
use the new Typ 901 210hp flat six-cylinder engine.
But familiarity with the flat fours and the worldwide
prevalence of spare parts suggested otherwise.
So approximately 130 chassis were built using the
Typ 587/3A 2.0liter, 180hp engines plus a handful
of six- and eight-cylinder prototypes.*

1965 Typ 904/8 Bergspyder
What it lacked in grace and style, it made up for in punch. This is the first of five Bergspyders—or open mountain-racers—that engineer Ferdinand Piëch ordered as the new head of engineering and development. Barely 130in long but with 240hp on hand, the car jumped— hence its nickname the Kanguruh.

victories—in the 2.0-liter-and-under categories—were no longer enough. As such, a progression of exciting racing cars appeared. And these brought results.

Butzi Porsche's lovely Carrera GTS was conceived and designed to accommodate racing versions of the Typ 901 six-cylinder production engine. Development problems delayed this through 1964 but in 1965, the first 904/6 coupes appeared, supplemented by Piëch's ugly, stubby, aggressive 904/8 Bergspyders ("mountain spyders," primarily for hill climb racing). These tiny 11ft. long, 1,154lb cars used Porsche's Typ 771 2-liter flat-8 cylinder 240hp engine. The first car was nicknamed *Kanguruh* because of its handling. In 1966, the striking Carrera 6s (Typ 906) appeared, quickly nicknamed the *Batmobile* by photographers who appreciated its gull-wing type doors. Sleek 906s raced at LeMans with aerodynamic tails more than two feet longer than normal *Batmobiles*.

Piëch remained interested in hill climbs. The 904 chassis was not efficient and so a tubular space frame and slightly longer wheelbase evolved into the Typ 910 in 1966. For hill climbs, the 910s continued to use the Typ 771 engines first seen in the 904/8; versions of the Typ 901 flat six were used for endurance races. With Hans Herrmann and Jo Siffert driving, a 6-cylinder 910 finished 4th overall at the Daytona 24-hours, and Gerhardt Mitter and Scooter Patrick finished third at Sebring behind two 7-liter Ford GTs. Typ 906s were sold to privateers from the beginning, but Porsche decided against selling 910s. As factory entries in prototype classes,

1965 Typ 904/8 Bergspyder
Porsche flat eight-cylinder Typ 771 displaced 1,991cc from 76x54.6mm bore and stroke. Four Weber 48 IDF carburetors and 10.4:1 compression produced 240bhp at 8500rpm. From a standstill, the Kanguruh *reached 100km/h in 4.8sec. Driver's with sufficient courage topped 150mph.*

the 910s did not compete directly against customers in 906s who would have chafed at the cost of needing a new car to remain competitive each year.

In 1967, Piëch, intrigued by the 911, created four prototypes and twenty production versions of a lightweight racing Typ 911R. These innocuous white coupes used lighter body and window panels. They became development test beds for engine and transmission variations. Between 1967 and 1970 911Rs won countless races, rallies, and world endurance records running with carbureted or fuel-injected 906 engines and even Sportomatic semi-automatic transmissions.

Eight-cylinder racing engines were used in 1967 in the Typ 907s. These also achieved 225

numerous overall victories. Hans Mezger developed their 2.2-liter versions from his complex Grand Prix engine, replacing Weber carburetors with Bosch mechanical fuel injection. The 907's slightly smaller bodies evolved from lessons in aerodynamics learned from the 904, 906, and 910. The Typ 908s appeared in 1968. Powered by Mezger's 3.0-liter flat eights, the 908s continued Piëch's assault on overall victories. Porsche produced 908 long-tail coupes for endurance races such as Daytona and LeMans and followed with two short-tail versions, the 908/2—known as *Flounder* for its undulating body—and the 908/3, which introduced wind-tunnel aerodynamics to Porsche racing. The stubby 908/3 soon showed its cleanly cut, truncated tail to the racing world.

The 908/3s ran away with events such as the Targa Florio, the 1000km of Nurburgring, and many others. Yet the factory 908L lost the 1968 LeMans (third behind Swiss racers Rico Steinemann and Dieter Spoerry in their own 907) by 100 meters after 24-hours to a five-liter Ford GT. A Federation International Automobile (FIA) Group 5 and 6 rule change for 1969 was meant only to extend the life of existing cars such as Ford's GT40 and Ferrari's 250LMs, 330s, and 512s. However, Piëch found a loophole. Through it, he served notice on the rest of the racing world.

1967 Typ 911R

Engineering chief Ferdinand Piëch used the 911R to answer questions: how light can we make it, how hard can we push it, how long will it last? Its highest achievement: 12,505 miles in ninety-six hours at more than 125mph, plus sixteen other records during the same run. In 1968, a specially constructed car won the Marathon de la Route using the Sportomatic transmission. And in 1969, another car using a special fuel-injected prototype engine won both the Tour de France and the Tour de Corse.

1967 Typ 911R, right

Standard fare for the "production" 911R was the Typ 901/22 2-liter flat six, with bore and stroke of 80x66mm. Using two Weber 46IDA3C carburetors, 210hp at 8000rpm was claimed. Free-flow resonators gave the 911R a distinctive exhaust note.

1972 Typ 911S Targa
When the last 356C cabriolets were produced in 1965, Porsche was left without an open car. California distributor Johnny Von Neumann proposed a prototype Bertone-designed spyder, but he knew the 911 chassis was not stiff enough. While Bertone fabricated, Ferdinand Alexander "Butzi" Porsche, designer of the 911, solved the problem with a built-in roll bar.

Hans Mezger reviewed drawings for the Cisitalia 12-cylinder engine from Gmünd. From this he designed Porsche's Typ 912, its most formidable engine ever. This was the 4.5-liter, air-cooled, fuel-injected flat 12-cylinder for the Typ 917 racing cars. The new rules for Group 5 and 6 required a "production" of twenty-five cars or more with a maximum engine size of 5-liters. Ferrari and Ford each had plenty of 512s and GT40s. Racing fans loved the battle between Modena and Dearborn, and track owners loved full grandstands. The FIA hoped to keep everyone happy while saving manufacturers the cost of developing new cars. The FIA never expected Porsche's 917s.

1972 Typ 911S Targa

Porsche's racing and high-performance models have frequently been named in honor of the company's first international victory in Mexico at the Carrera PanAmericana. When time came to name Porsche's steel-banded, stiffer cabriolet, Press Chief Evi Butz suggested honoring company wins in Sicily at the Targa Florio.

The twenty-five 917s—assembled only enough to pass FIA inspection—came together hastily. There was no track or wind tunnel testing. After the cars were homologated they were dismantled to undergo further development, as was usual with any racing car. A few prototypes were taken out for track testing. Their long tails revealed a diabolical nature. The design team directed by Helmut Flegl had taken each previous successful design, the 906, 907, and 908, and moved on. But the longtail designs had succeeded by luck. Under hard acceleration the 917's nose tended to lift. Worse, under braking, its elongated teardrop shape provided too little downforce, and the rear end lifted, whipping the back of the car. Seasoned racers quickly nicknamed the 917s. Brian Redman called it the *Widowmaker*, Gerhard Mitter named it the *Ulcer*, and Vic Elford referred to it as a "monster."

A mid-season test session at Zeltweg, Austria, revealed the solutions. The Canadian-American Challenge (Can-Am) racing series in North America gave birth to 917 Spyders with lines based on the 908/3. At Zeltweg, a Spyder using the coupes' chassis, engine, and drivers, lapped the track four seconds quicker than the coupes. It had none of the coupe's evil handling. Gulf Oil provided sponsorship for the 1970 European season and team Manager John Wyer, John Horseman and others joined Flegl in creating a solution at Zeltweg. The teardrop end of the first coupes was filled out to match the fuller, stubby end of the Spyder; the 917K (for Kurz, German for short) was born at Zeltweg and the problems were largely solved. Engine and gearbox reliability was improved as well and the 917s began winning races before the end of 1969. Ferdinand Piëch's goal of the Manufacturer's World Championship seemed within reach for 1970.

But the costs of developing and racing the 908s and 917s had grown unsupportable. A financial meeting revealed that 30 million DM had been spent on all forms of racing in 1969. In a shrinking economy, this was no longer possible for a family-held business. Piëch's dream could only come true through complete sponsorship from outside sources such as Gulf Oil. Factory racing development was stopped. Piëch's reason-for-being was taken away. A split occurred between the Porsches and Piëchs. Louise Piëch returned to Salzburg to concentrate on her Austrian distributorship; from there Ferdinand could continue to campaign 908s and 917s as a privateer through Porsche Salzburg. With Martini & Rossi sponsorship, he raced against the factory team in Gulf Oil colors.

1972 Typ 911S Targa
U.S.-specification 911S 2.4-liter engines used mechanical fuel injection. The 84x70.4mm Typ 911/53 flat-6 cylinder engine produced 190hp at 6500rpm, and the car weighed 2,365lb. In 1972 only, the dry sump oil filler was outside (below the Targa bar) on the passenger side. Too often, gas station attendants filled the sump with gasoline.

1972 Typ 911S Targa

Ironically, critics first called the stainless steel Targa band too flashy. Butzi Porsche responded that it was a structural element and no apology would be made for it. The customers should see improvements for which they reap benefits. The lightweight top removed easily and folded for storage.

Long-tail 917s were still run where higher top speed was more important than tight handling through corners. For LeMans 1970 and 1971, the Gulf team and the Martini-sponsored Salzburg team ran the 917Ls as well as shorter K-coupes. Piëch fulfilled his own dream for uncle Ferry Porsche's company: when 917 victories were tallied up, Porsche had won the World Championship of Makes both years.

In North America, Porsche won the Can-Am series with its Porsche+Audi-entered 917P+A Spyders. Engines grew from the 4.5-liter, 580hp coupe versions to 4.9-liters with twin turbochargers, producing 1000hp. In 1971 Mark Donohue and George Follmer, racing L&M-sponsored 917-10s for team owner Roger Penske, claimed the championship. For 1972, Donohue with Sunoco-sponsorship dominated the series in the Typ 917-30s. Using a 5.4-liter twin-turbocharged flat-12 with 1,300hp, the 240mph Porsche swept the series.

But the joys—and excesses—of the late 1960s and early 1970s caught up with motorsports. A worldwide recession, aided by the formation of the Organization of Petroleum Exporting Countries (OPEC), brought high-powered automobiles and racing into critical focus. Porsche sales in 1969 (15,000 cars

worldwide) shrunk one-third in 1970, to 10,000. U.S. distribution was reorganized with the introduction of Audi. Porsches previously were sold in facilities often owned by Volkswagen dealers. Now VW dealers had to build separate showrooms to sell Porsche and Audi. (It was to promote this relationship that the 1970 Can-Am entry was named the 917P+A).

"The cockpit was so narrow relative to the chassis—which was comparatively wide—we were sitting barely to the right of the centerline. The bit of the car that was reserved for the driver was pretty small!"

—Vic Elford on the 907K, from Porsche Legends

1968 Typ 907K, opposite page

Ferdinand Piëch's new 907 moved the driver to the right side where the 906 and 910 still drove on the left. Much smaller than the 910, the 907 with its fighter-plane-type cockpit offered a 25 percent decrease in aerodynamic drag. Barely 159in long overall, it stood only 36.2in tall. The 907's Typ 771/1 flat-eight displaced 2,195cc with 80x54.6mm bore and stroke. Bosch mechanical fuel injectors helped produce 270hp at 8600rpm. With the Typ 907 five-speed transmission, the combination proved good for nearly 185mph in the 1,265lb two-seater.

1969 Typ 908LH, next page

One of three langheck (longtail) 908s, these 3-liter flat eight-cylinder powered prototypes produced 350hp and topped 200mph on the Mulsanne Straight at LeMans. The rear wings were controversial but required to tame a flight-prone rear end. The 908 came third to Ford's 5-liter GT40 in 1968—by a scant 100 meters after twenty-four hours.

1969 Typ 917K, previous page
Wearing 1970 Gulf Oil colors, the K benefited from aerodynamic improvements reached at the end of 1969 that eliminated a terrifying lift that occurred when drivers came off the gas pedal. The 917 was Porsche's answer to a new FIA ruling favoring existing cars, but the FIA never expected Porsche would produce a new car to take advantage of the rule change.

1969 Typ 917K, above
Hans Mezger's Typ 912/00 engine was the first version of his air-cooled flat 12-cylinder and produced 580hp at 8400rpm. The 4.5-liter, 85x66mm bore and stroke engine fitted dual overhead camshafts and used Bosch mechanical fuel injection.

1970 Typ 917L

English racer Vic Elford called the longtail a "monster" but loved it. He tamed the monster well enough to take it along Mulsanne flat out at 245mph at night in the rain without lifting from the gas through the "kink," a slight right bend. The 917s exemplified the coming of the end of an era in motorsports with no limits.

1970 Typ 917L
For Ferdinand Piëch, the 917 represented an all-out assault on the World Championship rather than merely another class victory. The undulating shapes were invented by design engineer Eugen Kolb and were graced, like fine art pieces, with Styling Chief Tony Lapine's memorable paint schemes.

"You couldn't change your mind if you'd committed it to a corner. If you'd made a mistake, you were pretty likely to have an accident."

—Vic Elford on the 917 long tail, from Porsche Legends

1972 Typ 917/30, next page
Mark Donohue made Can-Am history with the Sunoco 917/30, and Herbert Müller raced the InterSerie, a kind of European Can-Am series, with Martini-Rossi sponsorship. Running the Typ 912/51 engine—Hans Mezger's chef-d'oeuvre—Müller and Donohue had twin turbochargers and intercoolers at their disposal. With the boost up, nearly 1,300hp propelled the 1,760lb spyders .

243

Chapter Three

TAKING THE TURBO TO THE STREETS

In September 1969, Porsche introduced the Typ 914 at the Frankfurt Auto Show. Conceived in 1966 as a sports car project for Volkswagen, the mid-engine car came back to Porsche when VW management changed in late 1968. Porsche continued developing the car as a replacement for its 912. Derided in the European press as the Volks-Porsche, it used the VW411's 80hp 1.6-liter engine. A stronger version, the 914/6, used Porsche's 2-liter 110hp 911T engine. Over its lifetime, 3,353 of these 914/6 models sold. The 914/6 GT used Typ 901/25 engines. The oil cooler from the 910 was mounted in the nose, the suspension modified, and the chassis was stiffened. This work could be done at Zuffenhausen or pieces could be purchased from local dealers and installed by racers themselves. Factory entries won the 84-hour Marathon de la Route, and long-time Parisian distributor SonAuto won GT class at LeMans in 1970, averaging just 19mph less than the winning 917K. An extremely limited-production Typ 916 appeared in 1972. The cars used a 190hp 911S engine in a body with a welded-in-place steel roof and were only offered to Porsche family and friends. Just eleven of these mid-engine, leather-upholstered, $12,900 coupes were built in 1972.

In the boardroom another reorganization had occurred. Soon after the Piëchs and Porsches withdrew from actively running the company, Ernst Fuhrmann returned. The brilliant creator of the Carrera four-cam engine for the 356s had left Porsche in 1956 when further advancement seemed unlikely. After 15 years running another company Fuhrmann was hired to come back to Porsche as its Technical Director. He is an enthusiast who loves racing and high-performance engines. But he returned to a company where budget constraints severely limited what was possible, where a world economy doubted the need for expensive two-seat high performance cars, and where U.S. safety concerns became a consideration in future product design.

Porsche engines had grown from 2.2-liters to 2.4-liters. Plans existed to replace the

1973 Carrera RS, opposite page
A total of 1,580 Carrera RS 2.7 models were sold, 528 as Lightweight coupes in order to qualify it for racing. The engine, Typ 911/83, produced 210hp at 6300rpm and was bored out to 90x70.4mm. Front and rear bumpers, rear decklid, and burzel ducktail spoiler were fiberglass, and the interior deleted all sound deadening material.

1970 914/6 GT, above

Porsche's long-time French distributor, SonAuto, entered the 1970 LeMans with this factory-built 914/6 GT, driven to first in GT class, sixth overall, by Guy Chasseuil and Claude Ballot-Lena. Averaging 99.3mph, they covered 2,382.5 miles on one set of tires and brake pads.

1970 914/6 GT, right

Porsche created a virtual 906 racing engine for the 914/6 GT with the Typ 901/25. Its 80x66mm bore and stroke displaced 1,991cc, and two Weber 46IDA3C carburetors helped achieve 220hp at 7800rpm. Cylinder heads featured larger valves, a more aggressive camshaft, and twin-plugs with transistorized ignition.

1970 914/6 GT, left
FIA regulations required that Gran Turismo entries carry a "passenger" seat with safety harness. Otherwise, the interior was a 914 stripped of all weight and nonessentials. The Typ 901 5-speed gearbox was fitted.

1970 914/6 GT, below
Front and rear deck lids and bumpers were plastic while the wide fender flares were steel welded directly to the structure. Wider wheels, 6x15s front and 7x15s rear, were responsible for grip and cornering during 1970 LeMans, which ran much of the night in the rain.

1970 Typ 911ST

The ST's in rally trim used the Typ 911/20 2.2 liter with 84x66mm bore and stroke. With Bosch mechanical fuel injection, the engines produced 180hp at 6500rpm. This 1970 ST was lightened before assembly using aluminum for the rear deck lid and doors and fiberglass for the front and rear bumpers and hood. It weighed barely 2,002lb. Three entries plus a spare were produced, this one winning Monte Carlo in 1970 with Bjorn Waldegaard driving and Lars Helmers as navigator.

911. But Fuhrmann knew that many Porsche buyers were repeat customers. These loyalists liked the car. He was not at Porsche when Piëch's 911Rs stretched the limits of the 911. But he knew the cars and had read the newspapers. It only remained for Fuhrmann to pump enthusiasm back into the product. Racing in Group 5 and 6 was out of the question, but competing in production-based Group 3 and 4 still earned newspaper coverage that brought buyers to the dealers.

So in October 1972, Porsche unveiled its 2.7-liter Carrera RS at the Paris auto show. It was jazzed up with script lettering along the sides and a new *burzel* (ducktail) on the rear deck lid to suggest its racing heritage. Sound deadening, undercoating, and interior insulation were deleted. Lightweight panels were used for front and rear deck lids. The engine, virtually new, produced 210hp (the 1972 production 911S used the 180hp 2.4-liter engine) and could push the RS to 155mph. Porsche had to build 500 to qualify for Group 4. All 500 sold at the Paris show. Another 500—with the insulation materials replaced that were deleted to qualify the 2,117lb lightweight racer—were built and sold immediately. Final sales counted 1,580 2.7 RS cars sold, a number that qualified it for Group 3 racing. Porsche's total worldwide sales returned to 15,000 cars that year.

For Group 4 the racing engineers produced a full-competition RSR version with 300hp. It won its very first race in February 1973, the Daytona 24-hours, only five months after the Paris show. But due to emissions and safety standards, the 2.7 RS was not legal in the U.S. It was not until 1974 that a 174hp

1973 Carrera RS
Series production began in October 1972 for the Carrera RS 2.7-liter coupes, meant to return Porsche to racing without the costs of developing prohibitively expensive prototypes like the 917s again. The production versions, Group 4-legal, quickly led to RSR competition versions, raced days and nights through the next three years.

U.S. version was available to buyers. Not only was the engine modified, but 5-mph-impact bumpers and door side-impact reinforcements had to be installed as well.

The frontal impact of OPEC hit in 1974. Porsche reduced production to a three-day work week as output slipped below 9,000 cars including 914, 911S, and Carrera models.

Again, the life and future of the company—and the 911—were threatened. But Ernst Fuhrmann had started life as an engine designer, and he looked to the engines for the company's salvation. He saw that a legacy of wealthier times was the turbo that had brought success in the Can-Am and the Inter-Serie, Europe's version of the races. It seemed natural to him to incorporate this device that improved power output so greatly yet actually quieted the engine. The Typ 930, intro-duced in late 1974, shoe-horned a tur-bocharger into a jammed engine compart-ment and provided 260hp at 5500rpm. Europe got production cars in March 1975 while U.S. certification (emissions and safety again) delayed arrival until year's end. The *"burzel"* from the 2.7 RS was enlarged into a "whale tail" flat wing for both the 930 and the Carreras.

The U.S. market remained crucial. While emissions standards deprived the 911S and Carreras of 10hp (and an additional 5hp off for California-bound cars), the factory fitted other standard features and even priced the U.S.-bound cars lower than those destined for the German market. With the 930's U.S. arrival—renamed the 911 Turbo Carrera to replace the normally aspirated Carrera—U.S. sales exceeded half of all Porsches sold.

SACHS
Dick Barbour RACING
6
SACHS
CLUTCHES & GAS SHOCKS
GOODYEAR
GOODYEAR

New Engines in New Locations

From the early days, Porsche was the research and design arm for Volkswagen. A certain portion of VW's budget was allocated to Zuffenhausen and to Weissach (opened in 1971) for development of new models. When Fuhrmann returned to Porsche in 1971, the engineers had already begun work on a new VW project, EA425, a front-engine water-cooled fastback sport car. As with the Typ 914, events conspired to scuttle VW's ambitions. Political and economic considerations made the car too valuable to kill and EA425 reverted to Porsche to become its Typ 924. Production began in November 1975 using the 125hp fuel-injected VW engine. When the 924 was turbocharged for the 1979 model year, it boosted power to 170hp and the car performed nearer to expectations. (Ironically, at that time, emissions standards had so tightly hamstrung the turbo 930 that U.S. sales were discontinued.)

1980 Typ 935K3, opposite page
One of racing's most successful conglomerates merged Porsche of Weissach with Erwin Kremer of Cologne to produce a product managed and operated by Dick Barbour of California. In 1980, the Barbour Racing 935K3 took first in Group 5 at the Nurburgring 1000km and first in IMSA's GTX class at LeMans.

In late 1975, as the 924 and 930 became available to dealers, a racing version of the 930, the Typ 935, showed the motorsports world that Porsche was very much alive. Two factory-entered 935s, using a new turbocharged 2.86-liter flat-six with air-to-water intercooling, Bosch fuel-injection, and twin-plug ignition, were prepared for the 1976 racing season in Group 5. The 2,134lb cars had 590hp at 7900rpm to propel them to a few early—and encouraging—victories.

Racing engineer Norbert Singer was project manager for the 935, his second racer for Porsche. He was a master at reading and interpreting the FIA rules. For 1977 a change favored a competitor—until Singer understood that it did not prohibit him from making the same change and lowering the 935 by several inches. In 1977 Porsche began selling versions of the cars, the 935/77 (with 1976 specifications), to independent racers. Private teams such as Erwin Kremer in Cologne, Germany, and Bob Garretson and Dick Barbour in California bought cars and immediately modified them to try to beat the factory team in European and U.S-International Motor Sports Association (IMSA) events.

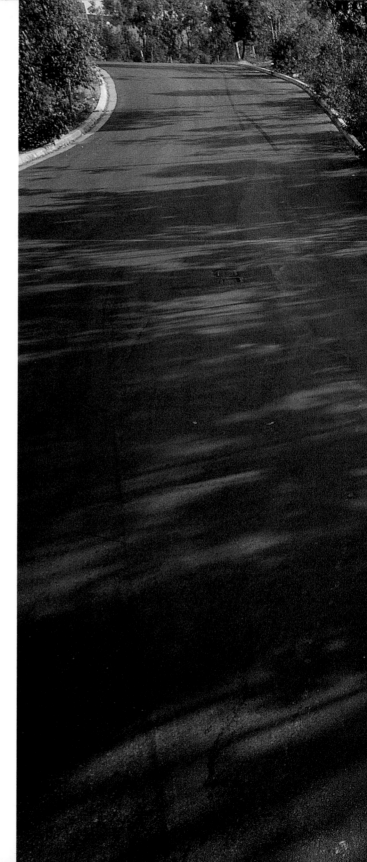

1980 Typ 935K3
Erwin Kremer performed more than 100 changes on the 935 including obvious bodywork modifications. Ekkehard Zimmermann of Design Plastic Company specified Kevlar for Kremer's new body pieces. He also added "fences" along the fenders to control airflow over the car.

For 1978 a new FIA rule allowed "aerodynamic appliances" which meant to Singer a whole new nose, tail, fenders, and doors and which meant to the world *Moby Dick*. FIA inspectors were stunned. Rules intended to ban such creations somehow had encouraged them. *Moby Dick* spawned a generation of aerodynamic appliances. Others copied the bodywork, and variations of *Moby Dick* quickly appeared. Then Kremer produced his legendary 935K3 and won eleven of twelve German National Championship races in 1979. Beginning in 1980, Kremer sold entire cars as well as kits to convert 935/77s into K3s. Dick Barbour bought a car and won IMSA's championship in 1980.

In mid-October 1975, while Weissach labored over the 935s, Ernst Fuhrmann asked Norbert Singer to consider the prototype regulations for Group 6. Fuhrmann suggested that old spare parts from the 917s could be "adapted". With eight months until LeMans and with French Renault and Italian Alfa-Romeo team prototypes already in preparation, Fuhrmann wanted again to be in the hunt—even while watching the budgets.

Some parts worked but much of the Typ 936 was completely new, produced almost overnight. When 1976 ended, the 520hp 3.0-liter, 1,540lb spyders won four outright

victories out of eight starts—including LeMans. This gave Porsche and Fuhrmann the championship for Group 6. The next year, the 936/77 won again at LeMans. And in 1981, in its final appearance, Fuhrmann's thoroughly updated five-year-old car developed from 917 parts, the 936/81, won again at LeMans.

The 924s raced as well. A 924 Carrera GT was introduced at the 1979 Frankfurt Auto Show. With a turbocharged, intercooled version of the 2.0-liter Audi-based in-line four-cylinder engine, the GT boasted 210hp. To qualify for Group 4, 400 were sold. Then fifty models of a higher-tuned Carrera GTS were produced and sold, followed by sixteen of the Typ 924 Carrera GTRs. In LeMans trim, these most-modified cars weighed 2,083lb, 800lb less than street 924 Turbos. With 375hp engines they reached nearly 180mph on Mulsanne. Porsche entered three GTRs in 1980, painted with the flags of its primary markets, Germany, the United States, and the United Kingdom. After twenty-four hours, much of it in rain, the 924s were still running. The best finish came from the German-flagged

1980 Typ 935K3
Plumbers nightmare—or brilliant design— Kremer used the flat fan and managed to fit an air-to-air-intercooler into cramped space as well. The endurance-tune 3-liter K3 engine produced 780hp at 8000rpm with twin KKK turbochargers. In LeMans dress, without fluids, the K3s weigh 2,270lb.

1980 Typ 935K3
Kremer stiffened the chassis through triangulated roll cage members to each shock absorber tower. The 935s started out with a production 911 steel chassis to which an aluminum tube roll cage was fitted, surrounded with fiberglass or Kevlar bodywork. Barbour race preparation was extremely tidy.

1981 B.F.Goodrich 924 Carrera GTR
In June 1982, Porsche had again won LeMans, this time with its new 956. Minutes later, B.F. Goodrich's one year old 924GTR #87 finished fifteenth after 2,307.9 miles at 96.2mph. The sister car, #86, retired in the eleventh hour. Racing in Group 5, Porsche produced only sixteen GTRs, after homologation was met with 400 924 Carrera GT models and fifty GTS versions.

car at sixth overall. The 924GTRs returned in 1981, entered by American tire maker B.F.Goodrich to promote a new high-performance street radial. Two factory 924s were entered as well; one of them was a 2,196lb 924 Carrera GTP that offered a hint of what production Porsche buyers could expect in the future. It was powered by a new 2.5-liter Porsche-designed, in-line four-cylinder engine with 410hp at 6500rpm. The GTP, precursor to the Typ 944 (and now generally referred to as the 944 GTP), finished seventh overall behind Fuhrmann's 936/81.

Both the 924GTP and the 936/81 ran new engines developed from other projects. The 936 used an engine spun off an ill-fated assault on the U.S. Indy car series, while the sixteen-valve 944 engine was one-half of a 5.0-liter V-8 water-cooled engine destined for the luxurious Typ 928 coupe.

As early as 1971 there was concern in the U.S. about the handling characteristics of rear-engined cars. In meetings at Weissach, engineers recognized that if the U.S. began legislating automobiles, it would not outlaw water-cooled, front-engined, rear-wheel drive cars produced in Detroit. So in between other projects, Porsche engineers began to conceive and develop the Typ 928.

Design chief Tony Lapine felt obligated to retain the organic, roundness begun with Erwin Komenda's Gmünd coupes. He chal-

1981 B.F.Goodrich 924 Carrera GTR
The Audi-derived Typ 924GTR engine displaced
1,984cc with bore and stroke of 86.5x84.4mm,
producing 375hp at 6400rpm. The single large
KKK turbocharger and intercooler helped to fill the
engine compartment. To eliminate head overheating
problems, a modified water system began the flow
of cooled water directly at the rear of the block.

Handling had been tamed. A new level of luxury had been reached. A front-mounted 4.5-liter 90-degree V-8 offered European markets 240hp, while for the U.S., 225hp came out cleanly through catalytic converters.

Engineers worked to improve performance; engine size jumped to 4.7-liters and then to 5.0-liters in the 1985 928 S models. Dual-overhead cams and four-valves per cylinder increased power again in the 928S4 models for 1987. Production topped 5,400 cars. The S4 performed well: 5.7sec to 60mph and a top speed of 165mph was possible. By 1990, engine output had risen to 326hp for manual transmission versions of the 928GT, providing a top speed of 171mph.

1981 B.F.Goodrich 924 Carrera GTR
A simple, unadorned, single-purpose-built machine,
the 924 GTR was also, at 180,000DM, the most
expensive 924 ever sold. Paul Miller, Pat Bedard, and
Manfred Schurti shared the cockpit until their race
ended when a left-front wheel came off in the early
morning.

lenged the engineers to make the car body act as its own bumper. Fitting in a water-cooling system radiator required other considerations in car bodies previous unperforated. In 1975, engineer Helmut Flegl took over as project manager to continue chassis and drivetrain development. The 928, introduced in Geneva in March 1977, won rave reviews. Appearance was stunning. Performance was impressive.

1981 B.F.Goodrich 924 Carrera GTR

The GTRs hit 180mph along Mulsanne racing on shaved street radial tires. The speed and power were held in check by brakes adapted from the 917 at front and 935 race cars for the rear. The cars *weighed 2,196lb without fuel or driver. The bodywork hinted at the production Typ 944 already in development.*

1984 Porsche 928S
The 928 was introduced in the fall of 1977, powered by a water-cooled 240hp 4.5-liter V-8. In 1980, the 928S came along with 4.7-liters and a small rear wing to clean up the aerodynamics. By 1985, with the 5.0-liter four-valve engine, performance at last matched the looks.

"Who has the right to define a Porsche only as a rear-engine, air-cooled car? Just because the first two cars were this, can we not grow? Do we not evolve?"

—Ernst Fuhrmann on the 928, from Porsche Legends

Chapter Five

RACING: TRIALS AND TRIUMPHS

Jo Hoppen, Porsche+Audi division competition director for Volkswagen of America had been one of the former guiding lights behind the 1971 and '72 Can-Am successes. In 1978 he visited Ernst Fuhrmann on behalf of American privateer Ted Field who wanted to take Porsche to Indianapolis. It struck Hoppen and Fuhrmann as a good promotional opportunity. The water-cooled-head engine from the Typ 935/78 *Moby Dick*, later used in the Typ 936/78 spyder, was the right size for Indy rules. Field had a Parnelli chassis proven and ready to go. It would require some work but they all reasoned that it could be accomplished by May 1980.

But no one imagined that the United States Auto Club (USAC) was about to be overtaken by Championship Auto Racing Teams (CART), an organization made up of racing team owners, not track owners and promoters. To other competitors, Porsche always represented a serious challenge. Rac-

1990 Porsche March 90P, opposite page
Porsche's Indy engine had an 88.2x54.2mm bore and stroke and produced 725hp at 12,000rpm. It was a dual overhead cam, four-valve-per-cylinder design with a single turbocharger and dual waste gates. Boost was limited to 45in of mercury (3.2 bar) through the pop-off valve atop the intake manifold.

ing history proves that rules could be changed to favor those already inside. So with barely a month to go before the 1980 Indy 500, the turbocharger boost allowance was changed, limiting Porsche to an uncompetitive level. Porsche had not sought an advantage over the other teams, but it had expected an equal opportunity. When that was denied, Porsche withdrew. The four Indy cars went straight into a warehouse.

Changes loomed on the horizon for both production cars and for racing. Similar factors influenced both. A new fuel crunch led to economic uncertainty and inflation. In 1978, the European Carrera was introduced in the U.S. as the 911SC; it was powered by a 3.0-liter 180hp engine. In 1980, 400 copies of a special Weissach commemorative coupe, filled with special trim and details, were produced.

In late 1981 at the Frankfurt auto show, a 930 cabriolet was shown. It would be another two years before the convertible—at first only available in white or red—would be sold. It was Porsche's first true cabrio since the last 356SCs in 1965. The open car was immensely popular. Despite an inflated economy, more than 21,800 cars were sold. Half went to the U.S. and half of those went to Califor-

1980 Interscope Indianapolis
Skilled IMSA-competitor Ted Field sponsored Porsche's first effort to conquer the Indianapolis 500. This attempt used a Parnelli chassis and an engine produced at Weissach. The 1,496lb car was 36.5in tall, 179in. overall, and rolled on a 104.5in wheelbase.

nia. The SC designation was dropped in 1984, replaced with the Carrera name as engine displacement increased to 3.2 liters and output rose to 200hp for the U.S. market, 240hp for Europe.

The same environmental and economic concerns that weakened U.S. engines affected FIA rules for racing when Group 5 and 6 were replaced in 1982 with Group C ("consumption"). This was racing meant to be fuel-efficient and environmentally responsible. Limits were placed on how much gasoline could be used in races of set lengths: 600 liters for 1,000km races, 2,800 liters for the 24-hours of LeMans. Engineers at Weissach met the challenge, introducing the Typ 956 in April and winning LeMans with it in June.

FIA specifications for driver safety and cockpit crushability led to an all-new chassis. Norbert Singer's solution was Porsche's first monocoque structure using steel, aluminum, and carbon fiber, surrounded by a Kevlar body. Singer also adopted Formula One technology: the 956 was Porsche's first ground-effects car. The 1,892lb cars used a twin-turbocharged/intercooled version of the 2.65-liter Typ 935/76 engine from the Indy project. It was detuned to 620hp at 8200rpm for endurance races. The cars won in 1983 and 1984 before regulations changed again.

Porsche returned to Formula One racing in 1983, providing its 1.5-liter, 80-degree V-6

1980 Interscope Indianapolis
The Typ 935/78 engine was fitted with water-cooled four-valve cylinder heads. Running a single turbocharger boosted to 54in of mercury (3.85 bar), the 2.65-liter V-8 produced 630hp at 9000rpm on methanol fuel. The heads were welded to the block. Caught by rule changes, it never turned a wheel in anger.

1982 Typ 956

Invented in March 1981 to campaign in the FISA's Group C category, the 956 was an immediate success, winning at LeMans 15 months later. It adopted parts of the ill-fated four-valve Indianapolis engine and the 2.65 liter used in the 1981 version of the 936. The 956 and subsequent Typ 962 went on to win at LeMans six times.

1990 Porsche March 90P, opposite page

Porsche attempted to compete in the CART series again in 1990 but met with frustration. Its 2.65-liter 90-degree V-8 never seemed perfectly mated to March's 90P aluminum-clad, composite materials sandwich monocoque chassis.

1990 Porsche March 90P

The Porsche-March was 183.5in overall on a 112in wheelbase. It was 78.5in wide, 36in tall, and weighed 1,550lb without fuel and driver (Teo Fabi or John Andretti). Two cars attempted the 1990 Indy 500, but neither finished.

TAG TTE-P01 engine for the Techniques Avant Garde McLaren team. The Formula One engine produced 630hp with twin-turbos at 2.5 bar boost. At the hands of drivers Niki Lauda and John Watson, the Porsche engines in McLaren's MP4/1E chassis struggled, but progress through the season was encouraging. For McLaren's 1984 MP4/2 chassis, boost on the TAG-P01 was raised to 3.2 bar and power increased to 750bhp. Changes and improvements yielded spectacular results: McLaren (with Alain Prost replacing Watson) won the constructors championship and Lauda won The World Driving Championship with Prost finishing second behind him. Between the

beginning of 1984 and the end of '87, Porsche and McLaren scored twenty-five GP victories. With those results Porsche once again yielded to the temptation of Indianapolis.

At the end of the 1987 CART season, the Typ 2708 2.65-liter 90-degree V-8 engine was mated to Porsche's own full carbon-fiber monocoque chassis. The engine produced 750hp at 11,200rpm at 48in (3.4 bar) of boost. Plagued by chassis stiffness problems, Porsche bought a March 88C chassis for the next year. Chassis problems continued until 1989's March 89P chassis put team driver Teo Fabi on the pole at Portland and left him first overall at Mid-Ohio. But reproducing the four-year run of success that Porsche had achieved internationally in Formula One proved elusive once again in U.S. Indy Car racing. The March 90P chassis and Typ 2708 engine, limited to 45in (3.2 bar) of boost, (producing 725hp at 12,000rpm) never quite worked perfectly. Porsche threw up its hands in frustration and withdrew from the series before the end of the 1990 season.

New IMSA rules dictated that a driver's feet must be behind the front wheel axle beginning with the 1987 season. This was adopted by the international governing bodies. The 956 wheelbase could not be lengthened because of the monocoque. As 956s crashed or teams ordered new cars, new Typ 962s were delivered as replacements. The factory raced its 962s at LeMans in 1987 and finished first, second, and third. And then Porsche withdrew, leaving endurance racing to its customers.

1990 Porsche March 90P

Teo Fabi pulled out of the pits during open practice before the first qualifying weekend. He qualified in 2min, 43.62sec, at 220.022mph. The cars were fitted with five-speed transmissions which failed on Fabi's car after 162 laps.

Chapter Six

STRETCHING THE ROAD CARS

In 1986, Porsche reintroduced the 911 Turbo to the U.S. market as a coupe, Targa, and a cabriolet, fulfilling the prophesy shown at the Frankfurt show in 1983. The Typ 959, a technology showcase also introduced at Frankfurt, was offered for public sale in 1987, albeit to a small, well-heeled crowd.

The 959 grew from the same inspiration that led Ferdinand Piëch to imagine the 911R and Ernst Fuhrmann to create the 2.7 RS and 930 Turbo. How far was it possible to take the 911? How fast? How advanced?

Peter Schutz, Porsche's then president, an American and a car lover, agreed with engineering chief Helmuth Bott that the 911 should go on and must go far. A prototype model, Typ 953, raced and won the 1984 Paris-Dakar rally. A Typ 961 road race version competed in Germany. When the four-wheel

1993 America GS Hardtop Roadster, opposite page
Porsche Customer Service, for customers of sufficient means, will delete undercoatings, adapt body panels from various models, install electronics suitable to monitor space flight, (and create power enough to assist it) and it will encourage the inventors, thinkers, and tinkerers from Zuffenhausen and Weissach to stretch their imaginations and to leap far beyond the normal production limitations.

drive six-speed Kevlar-bodied 959 appeared for sale in 1987, it accelerated to 60mph in 3.7sec and had a top speed of nearly 200mph. This was a production car meant for public roads. Only 224 were produced (including twenty-four prototypes to make certain that the ultimate 911 delivered on every promise). Porsche's unwillingness to bend to U.S. regulatory intransigence kept the car from American buyers except in the case of public museums and collections. Although fully legal elsewhere, for years these cars could be driven in the U.S. only with special permits on demonstration runs.

Just as the 959s were first sold in 1987, the 911 Speedster, another Bott/Schutz collaboration, was introduced at Frankfurt. Two prototype versions were blended into the final production model from which a limited run of 2,100 cars were finally sold.

The Typ 924 was replaced by the 944 in 1983, offered as a coupe and cabriolet; eventually a turbocharged version was also built. The 944 was replaced by the Typ 968 in 1991, fitted with a version of the six-speed transmission from the 959. At the same time, Porsche introduced the Typ 964 Carrera 2 and Carrera 4 models. These used a 3.6-liter

1988 Typ 959 U.S. Sport, above

The appearance of the 959 is testimony to styling chief Tony Lapine's ability to fulfill company president Peter Schutz and engineer Helmuth Bott's request for an ultimate 911 that would not betray the familiar lines. The body is steel, fiberglass, and Kevlar; the suspension is active and interacts with full-time active four-wheel-drive and anti-lock brakes. The car sold new for 430,000DM.

1988 Typ 959 U.S. Sport, left

The Typ 959/50 engine is 2.85 liters with 95x67mm bore and stroke. With electronic ignition and twin water-cooled turbochargers, 450hp is achieved at 6500rpm. Plumbing for the turbochargers is complex and fills much of the compartment.

normally aspirated air-cooled engine producing 247hp. Coupes, cabriolets and Targas could reach 60mph in 5.5sec and topped at 162mph. A Tiptronic transmission reinvented the Sportomatic semi-automatic gear box from the 1970s, but it was only available for the Carrera 2.

1989 Porsche 911 Speedster
Envisioned by Helmuth Bott, Tony Lapine, and Peter Schutz, the 911 Speedster adopted styling cues from other models and introduced the "camel humps" tonneau behind the seats. Around 2,100 were produced using the 3.2-liter flat-six mated to a five-speed transmission. Top speed was nearly 150mph.

1990 Porsche 930 Turbo Cabrio Flatnose
Working with engineer Rolf Sprenger's Sonderwunsch—special wishes—program in customer service, anything is possible if the client is willing and able. When the last regular production Typ 930 Turbo Cabriolet was purchased, the owner was intrigued by possibilities. Options opened up that had never before existed.

Special Wishes

The Customer Service department at Zuffenhausen has a program called *Sonderwunsch* (Special Wishes) that for decades has customized paint and interior trim to match clothing or even hair or eye color. It performs engine modifications and has detuned and modified racing cars like the 917K and 935 to street use. The final production turbo cabriolet, purchased by an American customer, set engineer Rolf Sprenger's Customer Service department reaching farther than ever before. The car was

fitted with acres of black leather and hundreds of never-before dreamed-of ideas and conveniences. A moisture sensor automatically raises the top and windows, arms the alarm, and notifies the owner of rain by remote pager.

Sprenger and his workers vowed never again to undertake anything so complex. But another opportunity arose. Inspired by Chief Stylist Harm Lagaay's Porsche PanAmericana built for Ferry Porsche's 80th birthday present, the owner of the final flatnose approached

1993 America GS Hardtop Roadster
Beginning with a Carrera 2 wide body cabriolet, the America GS roadster evolved. Incredibly, its removable steel hardtop has a fully retracting electric sunroof and

an electrically heated rear window. Electric contacts in the roof pillars and the roadster body provide the electricity.

1993 America GS Hardtop Roadster, above
The all-leather center console houses a graphic equalizer and numerous other spoiler, telephone, and security controls. Leather was specially dyed green and purple to specification, all supervised by Porsche chief stylist Harm Lagaay and executed by Rolf Sprenger's customer service staff.

Sprenger and *Sonderwunsch* again. Lagaay got involved. The result, after nearly four years work, was a kind of prototype for the 40th Anniversary issue of 250 America Roadsters. These were based on Carrera 2 wide-body cabriolets. The America GS (Grand Sport) Hardtop Roadster, challenged Sprenger's engineers. The idea was to recreate and update the 1950s sports cars that were driven to the track and raced all day. The GS's mechanical running gear is either Carrera 3.8-liter RS or RSR. It uses a racing Sportomatic gearbox, has no insulation or undercoating, no power steering or air conditioning, and has external electric kill switches. Carrera RSR Recaro racing bucket seats are leather covered. Its engineering piece-de-resistance is its removable hardtop that incorporates an electric sliding sun roof and electrically heated rear window.

1993 America GS Hardtop Roadster, previous page
The GS is fitted with a Carrera 3.8 RS engine and a racing version of the Tiptronic transmission to get nearly 300hp to the ground. Chassis and suspension modifications parallel those in the RS as well. Custom BBS 18in wheels hold Pirelli P-Zero tires all around.

1993 America GS Hardtop Roadster, above
The car's design was inspired by Ferry Porsche's eightieth birthday present, the PanAmericana showcar. It became a prototype for the 40th Anniversary America Roadsters. Production of this car took forty-four months.

1990 Porsche 930 Turbo Cabrio Flatnose
*From its flachtbau—flat nose—to its tea-tray tail,
nearly everything imaginable was touched on the car.
The build sheet specifying the options fitted to the car*
*ran to more than eleven pages. Leather abounds.
Stereo sound quality is better than some recording
studios. The car took two years to complete.*

1990 Porsche 930 Turbo Cabrio Flatnose, left
*Engine modifications are possible, although for the
U.S. market cars they are few and minor. Engine out-
put, aided by Bosch's Motronic Engine Management
System, is reportedly more than 450hp at 6500rpm.
A six-speed transmission from the Typ 959 was fitted
to a Quaiffe differential to take better advantage of
the engine's improved performance.*

1990 Porsche 930 Turbo Cabrio Flatnose
The already hand-built 930 cabriolet was virtually completely reassembled after chassis modification and suspension improvements were complete. Special instrumentation was added, some adapted from race cars, others from air craft. A moisture sensor will raise the top and windows, arm the alarm, and notify the owner by remote pager of the change in weather.

1993 Porsche 3.8-liter RSR, left
The new FIA-Super Cup contender 3.8-liter RSR sits in front of a 1967 911R, the car that inspired many of the "silhouette" racers that have evolved within bodies from production cars. Doors and front deck lid are aluminum.

Porsche announced in 1989 that the 911 Turbo would be discontinued. A new version on a new chassis would be introduced in the future, but the new car could accommodate neither the cabriolet body style nor the Typ 935 flatnose modification due to redesigned suspension geometry and engine oil cooling.

Just two years later, in 1991, the Turbo was reintroduced for 1992, using a 3.3-liter intercooled engine producing 315hp. At Frankfurt Porsche also introduced its Boxster, a mid-engine design study meant for possible production as an affordable Porsche (around

1993 Porsche 3.8-liter RSR
Derived from production cars, the center console parcel tray is retained as is a quite-standard-looking instrument panel. On-board fire-extinguisher lines surround the driver's Recaro competition racing shell. The car is limited by rules to a minimum weight of 2,464lb. Options include an air jack system.

1993 Porsche 3.8-liter RSR
Normal breathing seldom looks like this. The enormous air-intake covered with fine mesh allows engine sound to flood the cockpit. The mechanical crash and clatter of internal combustion at idle is such that inexperienced drivers wonder if the engine is self-destructing.

$40,000 U.S.). Porsche intends to counter the effective engineering and marketing competition from Japanese car makers. The Boxster, styled as a strict two-seater, is reminiscent of the Typ RS-60 spyder. Porsche also introduced the Carrera 3.8-liter RS and the RSR, meant for competition in the popular European Super Car Championships. The 2,462lb RSRs use a 3.75-liter 325hp Typ M64/04 flat-six with dual ignition. RSRs placed first in GT class at LeMans in 1993 and first, second, and third (eighth, ninth, and tenth overall) in 1994. The 300hp road version of the RS sells for 220,000DM in Germany and weighs only 172lb more than the RSR. But it is not yet legal in the U.S.

Beginning in 1992, Dauer, a specialty shop in Germany, began to modify 962 race cars for European road use. Enough of these were built that it qualified for GT class racing (Norbert Singer discovered that beneficial loophole). Porsche entered two Weissach-prepared Dauer 962LMs in the GT class. And following a long factory absence at LeMans, Porsche placed first and third overall in 1994. It was the firm's first victory there in seven years.

Over the past twenty-five years Porsche has suffered fits and starts. Hammered by the economy and challenged by aggressive competition, it has survived circumstances that have damaged other companies badly. Its problems are not over, but Porsche is still made up of passionate engineers deeply in love with the automobile. This great resource keeps Porsche at the top of the list of cars coveted by enthusiasts, admired by journalists, and respected by racers.

1993 Porsche 3.8-liter RSR

The two-deck plastic wing is a signature-piece of the racing RSR and its detuned road version RS. Unhappily for U.S. drivers, the RS is not legal. The 3,746cc RSR engine, Typ M64/06, produces 325hp at 6900rpm. The 5-speed transmission is connected to a 40-percent limited slip and, depending on the gearing, offers a top speed of at least 165mph.

INDEX